SHAKESPEARE MEMORIAL THEATRE

THE LORD ILIFFE G.B.E.

PRESIDENT OF THE SHAKESPEARE MEMORIAL THEATRE SINCE 1934

Shakespeare Memorial Theatre 1954-56

A PHOTOGRAPHIC RECORD

with a critical analysis by

IVOR BROWN

Photographs by Angus McBean

MAX REINHARDT

LONDON

First Published in 1956

The Publishers acknowledge with thanks the help they have received in the production of this book from the management of the Shakespeare Memorial Theatre, and in particular from
JOHN GOODWIN
the Theatre's Press and Publicity Manager

Designed by
WILL CARTER

Printed in Great Britain at
THE STELLAR PRESS
UNION STREET, BARNET

Bound by G. & J. KITCAT LTD
SHAND STREET, LONDON, S.E.1

SHAKESPEARE MEMORIAL THEATRE

STRATFORD-UPON-AVON

Incorporated under Royal Charter

Patron HER MAJESTY QUEEN ELIZABETH II

President The Lord Iliffe, G.B.E.

Chairman Sir Fordham Flower

Directed by Anthony Quayle, C.B.E. and Glen Byam Shaw, C.B.E.

General Manager and Licensee George Hume

THE BOARD OF GOVERNORS

Shakespeare Memorial Theatre
1954-1956

by IVOR BROWN

During recent years theatrical planning at Stratford has had a broadly-based intention. In Anthony Quayle's words Stratford has been seeking to provide both 'a testing-ground for the experienced actor to pit himself against the most exciting parts in our tongue' and a nursery 'where the young player can take his first uncertain steps towards becoming a classical actor.' Here is a clear and practical policy of double purpose. There is, however, an intermediate stage between those two functions of the Memorial Theatre : that is to introduce, in the 'exciting parts,' which are also the exacting parts, those who have got well beyond their 'first uncertain steps.' These, while still far from being old hands and vessels of experience, may be described as newly qualified to face post-graduate responsibilities and to meet the perils, as well as the pleasures, of the historic roles.

During the season of 1954 the accent was thus to be set on youth; not everything was likely to succeed entirely. But the public did not take a timid and conservative line. It did not decide that, because the cast lacked some of the previous star-clustered look, Stratford could be neglected for a year. There was a genuine response to the programme and to the company. The year's work, although it started early and continued late, never had any lack of support at the box-office whose takings were over 92 per cent. of capacity.

But before I go on to record the company's achievements and the critical assessments of 1954 I must look back to the winter of 1953.

At the close of that year two events occurred which could not be related in the last volume of this series of theatrical chronicles. One was the return in November of the Stratford Company which had been touring, with Anthony Quayle's leadership, in New Zealand and Australia; they had been away for nearly a year and had covered 30,000 miles. The reception had been most enthusiastic and rewarding and the reputation of the Stratford theatre had been enhanced. 1953, with its double undertaking at home and abroad, had been a year of far-flung and ambitious enterprise; the travelling company came back at the close of the Stratford season to find that Glen Byam Shaw's direction of the home-team in *Antony and Cleopatra*, with Michael Redgrave and Peggy Ashcroft in the title-parts, had been so much acclaimed that a London season of six weeks had been arranged with the co-operation of Jack

Hylton, and had already opened at the Prince's Theatre. One or two critics, who had given only a limited praise to the original presentation at Stratford, withdrew their hesitations, and one who thought that the first occasion had just ' missed ' decided that the London first night had been overwhelmingly successful. That was now a universal verdict of the public as well as of the Press. The Prince's Theatre, with a seating capacity of more than 1,700, is one of the biggest in London, but it was packed throughout the run (4th November to 15th December).

Immediately after that, in the early days of 1954, *Antony and Cleopatra* was taken to Holland, Belgium and France. It was a hustled tour and involved the organisers, as well as the players, in continuous toil and travel. They were two nights at the Hague, one at Amsterdam, one at Antwerp, two at Brussels, and six in Paris. As there was only one night without performance the strain on all was intense.

The response in Holland and Belgium was most cordial despite the fact that *Antony and Cleopatra* is not well-known and must be very difficult to follow in a foreign language. But there were some critical strictures in Paris. The Parisians are used to classics spoken and performed with a traditional respect for academic standards. *Antony and Cleopatra*, least academic of tragedies, was obviously a strange document to the first night audience and the huge, world-ranging sweep of Shakespeare's master-piece shocked some by its contempt for 'the classic unities,' while the intense and passionate realism of the performance, which had been so much applauded in Stratford and London, was regarded by the conservative judges in Paris with dismay. The discrepancy between English and French opinion actually evoked a leading article in the *Times*. Some jocose remarks by Parisian critics at the expense of the scenery and costumes – so unacademic, so untraditional! – were widely quoted. This helped to give a false impression that the visit to Paris was a disappointment both for the English players and the French public. The fact was far otherwise; the ' first night ' assembly was not typical of the Parisian taste and the Stratford company gladly acknowledged that a performance given specially for students was greeted by one of the most closely attentive and appreciative audiences encountered anywhere.

Back at Stratford in 1954 the work began early and with the happy knowledge that the finances of the Memorial Theatre were, despite a big investment in structural development during the previous years, extremely sound. There had been no re-course to State aid. During a period in which the pursuit of subsidies has become almost a national occupation Stratford has managed to remain independent and unaided. Would a programme with less direct box-office appeal suffice to continue this self-maintenance? And would the younger company sustain the standard of performance which had been established during recent years by players strengthened in their work by wider experience and enjoying the confidence given by past achievements and the possession of well-regarded names. The young players were wisely assisted by the fact that the plays chosen for them were young in spirit. All was immediately well. The advance bookings created a new record.

The start was made with a piece already in hand. This was *Othello*; the title-part was played by Anthony Quayle who had acted it with distinction through the long tour in the Antipodes: he had the same, and excellent, Desdemona in Barbara Jefford: he chose Raymond Westwell, who had played Roderigo overseas, to be his Iago. It was a promotion seemingly justified by the fact that Mr. Westwell had done consistently interesting work in a number of different roles. But he seemed, according to most critical opinion, to be, as was said of the curate Nathaniel in the heroic mummings of *Love's Labour's Lost*, 'a little o'erparted.' The story of *Othello* is hard enough to believe in any case, so idiotic is the Moor's refusal to use his brain and ask necessary questions. Iago must seem to be a man of really demoniac power, one who could put uncanny and overwhelming persuasion on a soldier of supposed intelligence. Raymond Westwell lacked the size and force for that. Onc of the happier pieces of casting in this production was that of Tony Britton as Cassius. Here was an actor who was consistently an asset to the Year of New Talents.

The reception of *Othello* had been on the whole rather chilly; there was rather more cordiality shown to *A Midsummer Night's Dream*, directed by George Devine and decorated by 'Motley.' But it was not a production to suit the romantics; there was no Mendelssohn. Roberto Gerhard's score was described by Alan Dent as 'a not unpleasing mixture of frogs croaking and the horns of elfland faintly blowing.' The fairies were closer to insects than to human beings, and the critics displayed a wide range of zoological fancy in their efforts to describe in animal terms the odd creature that was David O'Brien's Puck.

Fortunately the lovers' quartette, Barbara Jefford, Zena Walker, Tony Britton, and Basil Hoskins moved and spoke well for the anthropoid side of the cast, while royalty was gallantly and handsomely represented by Keith Michell and Jean Wilson. There was general enjoyment of the clowns and Anthony Quayle's Bottom, crew-cut, shy, wide-eyed, and bewildered in his high ambition, was a triumphant leader of a well-varied team of zanies. Leo McKern's Quince was a dry little darling of a man. The lovers of theatrical tradition could argue that both mortals and sprites were ill-met by this moonlight and with this kind of melody. But a young company must be expected to work out new notions and without doubt the production was enjoyed. Certainly the rustic mummery was made into as gay a riot as any lover of loud laughter could desire. The final bergomask, arranged by Pauline Grant, was a particularly happy caper.

Romeo and Juliet was directed by Glen Byam Shaw which ensured justice to the story and the text: no producer is less likely to play fantastic tricks with Shakespeare. He was hampered by the curious modernism of the set by ' Motley ' which gave small atmosphere of a sun-drenched, hate-soaked medieval Italy, but had a northern coolness and logic in its composition.

There was some admirable acting in the secondary roles: Keith Michell's Tybalt was a king of panthers, rather than of cats. Friar Laurence was richly humanised by Leo McKern and William Devlin made the most of old Capulet. The values of the main performances were variously assessed. It was agreed that Laurence Harvey had the looks, stature, and flow of feeling proper to Romeo, but his ability to match good speech with good looks was more in question. There was a warmer greeting for Zena Walker's Juliet, one of the youngest of our time. (She was only twenty when she played the part.) So she had real youth on her side as well as a good ear for the sound of a line. The common dilemma of all Juliets, that the child of the early scenes has to be the fully equipped tragedienne of the later ones, was met with ability, and it was not only the delight of the Midlands in a 'local girl making good' that allotted high praise to Zena Walker.

For Stratford this was being a difficult and troubled year as far as written criticism was concerned. The public were supporting the young team loyally, but there had been a good deal of rather depressing, deflating comment in the Press. It was insufficiently realised that experiment in the arts is both a necessary activity and an operation which is bound to involve some failures and disappointments. However, the general trend of the *Romeo and Juliet* notices was more encouraging than that of the reviews of the two previous productions, and it was being realised that the company had plenty of talent ripening amid the new opportunities.

The fourth production of 1954 was a revival, re-casting, and improving, of the previous year's *The Taming of the Shrew*. That which had gone well now went better. Keith Michell and Barbara Jefford were excellently cast as Petruchio and Katherine. They brought the right fantasy, as well as an authentic fury, to their strife and to the play within a play, which the producer, George Devine, rightly kept as such. He chose, as before, to round off the evening with a return to Sly and the Hostess by drawing on the other ' Shrew ' play of Shakespeare's time. A particular pleasure also was, once more, the richly detailed setting of a milord's mansion designed by Vivienne Kernot.

The verdict was generally favourable, but of course critics will never totally agree. What is a producer to think or do when the *Birmingham Post* congratulates the company on having learned to speak up, while *The Daily Telegraph* grumbles at 'a general tendency to shout.'? But Keith Michell, taking Petruchio to be a laughing cavalier as well as a tigress-tamer, and Barbara Jefford, dark, comely, and with a wit as well as a temper, were almost universally liked. The part of Bianca is not one that usually attracts much attention, but Muriel Pavlow succeeded in commending it to many judges. Harold Hobson in *The Sunday Times* came down sharply on the august author for the composition of 'this dull, brutal, ill-written, and indecent' play. Whether Shakespeare was less of an oaf and vulgarian than Mr. Hobson believes or whether the Stratford production was a clever feat of rescue-work and concealment for a product of oafish vulgarity, need not be discussed and cannot be settled. What was abundantly apparent was the common acceptance of 'The Shrew,' thus decorated and played, as being a most agreeable contribution to the Season of 1954. Perhaps we are too eager now to cover up what seems like brutish fun because we so much venerate its author. But we may surmise that Shakespeare, could he see the beauty and feel the light breeziness of a modern rendering of this early and uproarious piece, would be delighted to find that his crudities could be thus concealed, as it were 'Bottom translated.'

The fifth occasion of the year was Glen Byam Shaw's production of the tragical and comical and classical-satirical medley that is *Troilus and Cressida*. The eye was constantly delighted by a new and young designer, Malcolm Pride. His design for a Troy with a panoramic prospect of the plains beyond the City walls and outward to the Grecian quarters was widely acclaimed as an admirable venture in decoration. The acting had its blending of failure and success. The poignant and tragical side of this label-evading piece miscarried through the inability of Laurence Harvey to rise to the poetry of the entranced, betrayed, embittered Troilus. Thus Muriel Pavlow, strangely cast as his false and sensuous Cressida, was handicapped in her scenes of enticement and of treachery: yet she came out of her difficulties remarkably well.

The verbosity of Shakespeare's Greeks is always a menace to the onward drive of this intractable play: William Devlin was in fine voice as Agamemnon and thus fittingly concluded a season of excellent service in some less than helpful roles. Leo McKern dealt skilfully with the loquacity of Ulysses. Keith Michell as Achilles was suitably handsome of mien and contemptible of conduct. Tony Britton's charm, not easily disguised, made the assignation to him of the rancorous and odious Thersites impolitic. Anthony Quayle took Pandarus and worked out a memorable portrait of a lisping, giggling, intriguing old fribble.

The reaction to *Troilus and Cressida* was at least as cordial as could be expected in the case of a play always likely to puzzle more than it pleases. All were gratified by Mr. Pride's well-contrived union of external spatial effects with the pillars of the Trojan citadel and none could deny that Glen Byam Shaw's direction had been clear in its narrative and effective in its groupings and military manoeuvres. In conclusion it may be said that the challenge of 1954 had been met : there had been no defection of the public in the face of less glamorous casting than that which past seasons and the promise of 1955 were making familiar. There had been mistakes, sometimes of setting and sometimes in the assigning of parts. But it was certainly not true that Stratford had lost reputation and support among the Shakespearian public. It remained magnetic to myriads. If a foreign tour could not immediately be managed and there was no single production deserving the risk of a mid-winter season in London, such as *Antony and Cleopatra* had so rewardingly enjoyed in the previous year, then Stratford could still show to a larger audience its understanding of a Christmas comedy to suit the young idea. A. A. Milne's *Toad of Toad Hall* had been met with acclamation in previous Decembers beside the Avon, twice with Michael Hordern and once with Raymond Westwell in the name-part. For the Christmas of 1954 it was presented at the Prince's Theatre in London with John Kidd reviving his Stratford production. It had a successful holiday run. Leo McKern's playing of Toad was much appreciated for its vivid example of what inflation can do to a creature as well as to a currency.

The next year was to be one of double activity. It was to be ' the Oliviers' year ' at Stratford itself, while a European tour with a London season in the middle of it was to be led by Sir John Gielgud and Miss (now Dame) Peggy Ashcroft. The planning and execution of these ambitious undertakings, and especially of the foreign travel, naturally threw a great burden upon the administrative side and once more George Hume and his colleagues showed their capacity for coping with all the complex problems of finance, transport, and public relations, without whose effective solution the ' prestige ' achievements of a tour may easily be lessened or even lost.

Stratford opened with *Twelfth Night*, directed by Sir John Gielgud and decorated with conspicuous grace by Malcolm Pride, who, having in the previous year succeeded so well with his prospect of Troy, went on to do as much for the court and countryside of Illyria. Sir Laurence contributed a study of Malvolio which contradicted the tradition of a grandiose and flamboyant performance, rich in mockery of the man's pompous vanity: instead, there was a picture of a diligent, self-made domestic official, over-eager to keep order, a common, uneasy climber with a tortured lisp, one who, as J. C. Trewin wrote, looked as though he had lived on a diet of green apples. (Since, at the start of this season, there was a newspaper strike affecting London and most other towns, the criticisms were scanty or occurred later on in brief summaries of past events). Thus, the actor, not so much over-weening as under-weening, provided a plausible and untheatrical Malvolio, brilliant in many details. The risk of such a rendering, with its playing down of the steward's vastly swollen egotism, is to make the plot against him somewhat superfluous. Why bother so greatly to humiliate one who seemed to ask for only a light dismissal?

The comedy scenes lacked the usual boisterous attack. Michael Denison's Sir Andrew came best out of the somewhat tenuous fun, Alan Webb being cast too much against his natural type in the role of the robustly revelling Sir Toby. Vivien Leigh's Viola was an exquisite picture, but criticised for being somewhat cold and aloof. The story falters if Viola is not swiftly and overwhelmingly in love with Orsino. Maxine Audley's Olivia deserved all the compliments which the text awards to the lady, and Angela Baddeley's Maria had plenty of the gaiety sometimes lacking elsewhere. Expectation had been built high and the laughter, at least on the first night, was less than had been looked for; the original and incisive study of Malvolio was a surprise to those who took for granted the conventional pride of port and amplitude of flourish. But it was much valued by those ready for new approaches to the much-acted classic roles. Sir Laurence had avoided the usual stencil of the steward and had been, in a way that haunts the memory, unique.

While the Oliviers were preparing to be the Macbeths, there was a gallant production of *All's Well That Ends Well.* Stratford has to include the 'difficult' plays from time to time and this bitter comedy of the man-hunting Helena with its heavy-handed humours of the cowardly Parolles presented a producer new to such an office at Stratford, Noel Willman, with one of the least rewarding of Shakespeare's texts. Furthermore, the part of the objectionable and evasive Bertram is not one likely to be any actor's favourite. Michael Denison could hardly make the public like Bertram, but they could and did like the gallantry and address of his performance. Joyce Redman was a sweet-spoken and rather sing-song Helena, and criticised for want of metal in that determined woman's composition. Keith Michell made Parolles a source of smiles rather than of guffaws, while Alan Webb, in good voice as the King of France, seemed to have stepped from a Vandyke portrait. The decoration by Mariano Andreu was sumptuous in the Caroline manner: if play and performance were not always a satisfaction to the ear and mind, the eye was constantly gratified by a pageant of cavaliers. With 'All's Well' produced a duty had been done and the emphasis could be restored to work in which Shakespeare was himself again.

Macbeth, which followed, found scarcely a dissident voice as to the grandeur of performance in the title role. But less than justice was, in my own opinion, done to the vigour and clarity of Glen Byam Shaw's direction. Some were disconcerted because he began with his weird sisters in mid-air. But is not that commanded? The instruction comes immediately: ' Hover through the foul and filthy air.' One can, presumably, hover on solid ground, though the dictionary definition of this verb is, ' Hang, remain suspended ': but a coven of witches would certainly be airborne, if they could be, and Shakespeare may have contrived some suspension of his Sisters when the play was acted indoors. Mr. Shaw was fully justified in getting his witches aloft, and justified also in the detail of his cauldron-cookery and visions. Why do not critics, who snap at producers, read the plays before they start to be rude about effects that are plainly ordered ?

What mattered was the drive and directness of the story-telling. My own sensation was that of seeing this play afresh, with new eyes. I have often tried to read the text of a Shakespeare play as though I had never heard of it or seen it before, scouring away all previous opinions. It is extremely difficult, perhaps impossible, to achieve this innocence. But a good, faithful, unfussy, unpretentious production (or possibly a revolutionary one organised by a genius) can help in that direction. One did get a sudden and blessed sense of novelty. The merits of this *Macbeth* were properly in the acting and the free flow of the play's narrative. There was no nonsense. There was, on the other hand, vivid illumination.

Sir Laurence's own performance began quietly: the heroic patriot did not strongly assert his soldierly quality. But, once the hero was committed to villainy, the rendering was strenuous, lurid, unforgettable. It marched on to the desperate bewilderment of one for whom success has been a puzzle as well as a prize. It had desperation of the spirit as well as astonishing physical energy in battle: lastly, it had the ineffable weariness of the war that goes against a broken man. Nor did Sir Laurence forget that Macbeth, as Shakespeare made him, was one of the greatest poets who ever drew a sword and forgot to handle a pen. His voice was dismissed by one critic as inadequate to the majesty of the lines, being no more than ' a shrill and throaty tenor.' This was not the general verdict and certainly not mine. But what I especially noted was the subtlety of the facial play: every shade of feeling flickered across the mobile mask. But I was sitting close: much of this detailed artistry may inevitably have been missed further off.

Vivien Leigh's Lady Macbeth, red-haired, green-gowned, exquisite of aspect, hard of grain, was not, naturally, on the grand scale. But it is only the Siddons tradition that has persuaded us to believe that Lady Macbeth must be a tremendous theatrical figure. The character is tough, pertinacious, and has the personal magnetism that will mesmerically sway her hesitant hero to the supreme treachery and the risk of doom. These qualities Miss Leigh exactly provided. She looked the perfect queen for this king: for once the Macbeths, instead of appearing to be a couple of ' stars ' who dislike each other, were credible as man and wife. Here was the woman who could have so prevailed. And here, too, was another admirable couple, for Keith Michell's ardours and triumphs as Macduff were equalled by the intensity of Maxine Audley as his lady; her final scream of agony might have come from the echoing galleries of hell itself. Roger Furse's decoration was insufficiently praised: the fights arranged by Bernard Hepton and John Greenwood and carried out with breath-taking courage by Sir Laurence, Keith Michell, the Clan Chieftains, and other ranks were pugnacious and spectacular in the highest degree of histrionic combat.

It was a busy summer for Glen Byam Shaw, whose next charge was *The Merry Wives of Windsor*. He gave the Thames valley, with Motley assisting, a wintry look, even a Christmas-card setting. Why not, since, as I said, he reads the plays before producing them and had realised the weather of the play to have been raw and rheumatic ? But December on the stage was met with the sudden scorching of a torrid July in Warwickshire and there was general sympathy for Anthony Quayle, who had to swathe himself once more in Falstaffian wadding. Mr. Quayle conceded nothing to the weather and went gurgling and wheezing through the misadventures of the lickerish and liquorish knight with so much energy of comic invention that he must indeed have been ' hissing hot ' when the time came for his immersion in the Thames. Mr. Quayle by that hour of the night might have welcomed a similar fate in the Avon.

Keith Michell's Ford capably provided the expected rages. As the two ladies Angela Baddeley and Joyce Redman had their best parts of the season and their merriment was found authentic and infectious. Sir Hugh Evans was an unlikely part for William Devlin who made it a big success. Michael Denison's Caius was also much liked.

In mid-August came the Problem Child of the Folio, *Titus Andronicus*, from which Stratford had been flinching these eighty years. To signalise the first appearance there of this Horror-Tragic (or might one say the first emptying of this blood-bath into the Avon ?) a special programme was printed and bound in a black cover. Why not blood-red ? There was, in any case, no need for mourning. The theatre was not giving birth to a still-born child. Sir Laurence made Titus emerge as a true figure of tragedy, a fore-shadowing of Lear. Aaron, whose forthright and filthy wickedness might have seemed ludicrous, was played with such technical mastery and such a confident attack by Anthony Quayle that the all too nefarious Moor held the stage unsmiled at. I must confess that I went to Stratford for this occasion with a sinking feeling. I could not see so crude a collection of atrocities, such an assembly of Tussaud Terrorists, and such a feast of rape and mutilation being rescued from absurdity. Yet, at the close, an audience that had come with apprehension, rose at the players and cheered with more gusto than I have been used to hearing at Stratford, where after-curtain applause is by no means niggardly.

How did this happen? Peter Brook's production had been a masterpiece of salvage and a display of extreme cunning in the art of covering up. Shakespeare had been rescued from his 'prentice self and appeared almost as a matured master. This occurred despite the fact that the producer had culpably cut some of the few lines in the play that carry the obvious signature of the Shakespeare that was to be. (This was the more cruel to the part of Marcus, beautifully played by Alan Webb, who deserved to have his few plums left for him to pick.) Peter Brook's method was to drain off the rivers of gore, never to parade the knife-work, and, instead, to symbolise a wound with a scarlet ribbon. Lavinia hacked and gashed could still be an endurable sight and, since Vivien Leigh played the part, a very pretty one despite all her surgical and spiritual tribulations. The sensibility of the audience was thus spared without much mitigation of the plot: only at the very end was there complete concealment of an exceptionally grisly event.

But there had to be positive development of the play's merits as well as a cloaking and evasion of its faults. To this end Sir Laurence contributed nobly: he turned the part of the broken and bereaved veteran into an unforgettable utterance of despair. The role has some great lines,

> For now I stand as one upon a rock
> Environ'd with a wilderness of sea.

Sir Laurence was not only on a rock: he was a rock, the rock that is rent asunder with the dynamite of doom. So the audience were coaxed into believing that this was indeed a worthy play about a man both sinned against and sinning: if young and foolish in much of its writing for the melodrama market, it now became, under the persuasion of our strongest actor, a sounding-board of terrible, yet authentic, passions and of agonies monstrous but not beyond bearing by mankind.

Setting and music were both designed by Mr. Brook and both worked powerfully on the imagination. Here was the barbarism of Rome at war with Barbary. Yet here was a grandeur, as well as a savagery, of the primitive. So there was a proper background for Maxine Audley to glitter in ferocity as Tamora and for Anthony Quayle's Aaron to go leering and gloating on perdition's path. Also there was an atmosphere in which the tragedy of Titus could still be raised to a power higher than any which the public had foreseen. Thus Stratford, at last, completed, with a triumph that could hardly have been hoped for, its performance of the entire canon.

During the summer of 1955, while the productions just described were being presented at head-quarters, an English and European tour of the first importance was being made: this was begun early in June with a trial fortnight in Brighton and was continued with eight appearances at Vienna, four appearances at Zurich, five each at the Hague and Amsterdam, and two at Rotterdam. Then there was a return to London for a season at the Palace Theatre, which lasted from July 21st to September 17th. This was arranged so that visitors should not find London without any Shakespearian plays available, except at the hazard of the weather in Regent's Park. After that there were visits to Berlin, Hanover, Bremen, Hamburg, Copenhagen, and Oslo. From Norway the company returned to Newcastle and played a week there, followed by weeks in Edinburgh, Glasgow, Manchester and Liverpool. Finally these busy travellers wound up the year's work at Stratford itself by playing there from November 29th to December 17th, after the season of the ' Home ' company had ended.

The cast of the 'away' company was headed by Sir John Gielgud and Dame Peggy Ashcroft, and included Moira Lister, Helen Cherry, George Devine, Anthony Ireland, and Anthony Nicholls. The plays given were *Much Ado About Nothing* and *King Lear*. Sir John directed the production of the former and used the scenery and costumes, designed by Mariano Andreu, which had so delighted Stratford and London on previous occasions. The music was arranged by Leslie Bridgewater whose capacity for harmonising the airs to the text is one of the pleasures of the productions at the Memorial Theatre. This comedy, with no startling novelties in its presentation and with leading players whose work in it had already been very much appreciated, was an offering with no risks attached. That the ' merry war ' of Beatrice and Benedick would be fought with the utmost neatness of verbal fence was assured. Benedick is a part in which Sir John had displayed his perfect marksmanship with the arrow of a well-barbed line and Peggy Ashcroft had been no less adroit in returning the bolt with the most dexterous contrivance of stage archery. Here was the riposte of ' conceits ' that so delighted the Elizabethans with their keen appetite for word-play, and here were the best players of this pit-a-pat comedy and best speakers of a mannered prose and verse that our theatre contains. So far, so safe.

King Lear was another matter. George Devine, with Sir John assenting, audaciously determined that Europe should see something out of the ordinary and a

Japanese-American artist, Isamu Noguchi, was introduced to provide costumes and settings. The music and 'sound-score' were entrusted to Roberto Gerhard. For an international tour there was international talent enlisted as well as fresh conceptions entertained of mis-en-scène and productive method.

A programme note explained that 'Our object in this production has been to find a setting and costumes which would be free of historical and decorative associations, so that the timeless, universal, and mythical quality of the story may be clear. We have tried to present the places and the characters in a very simple and basic manner, for the play to come to life through the words and the acting.' That was the sensible purpose: the practice, however, caused much dismay, since the decoration was of so curious a kind that, in the general view, it interfered with the attention of the audience instead of concentrating it on the text and the performance. The critics, at any rate, found plenty of scope for ingenious similes when they came to describe the Noguchi clothings and settings. Lear arrived, wrote J. C. Trewin, not one to scoff lightly at anything Shakespearian or Stratfordian, with 'around his face a vast, drooping circlet of white horsehair, on his head what seemed to be an inverted hatstand, and in his grasp a decorated hearth-brush.' *Punch* wrote of 'women hideously wrapped, while the men wear deck-tennis rings for hats and variations on the cellular bath-mat over space-suits in heavy leather. No wonder Lear left a home in which he had to sit side-saddle on an abstract horse.' Anthony Cookman described Goneril and Regan as 'sinister geishas from *The Tea House of the August Moon*'. Allusions to space-fiction were common in the notices. On the other hand there was some approval from those critics who think that shocking the critics and the public is a salutary exercise. Richard Findlater in *Tribune* gave a whoop of joy because 'the Ancient British platitudes of stage tradition had been avoided' and 'the Modern British clichés of middle-class behaviour had been partly disguised.' But not only on the anti-bourgeois Left was this production praised: *Truth*, whose Conservatism is not to be questioned, in a long article of the highest praise for the acting as well as the decoration, decided that 'Mr. Noguchi has succeeded magnificently: it is not too high a praise to say that his ignorantly abused décors are fully worthy to go alongside the most rewarding interpretation of a great play by a great player that we are ever likely to see.' But the majority verdict was one of protest against innovation that had run, it was thought, to absurdity.

Of the acting there were also harsh things said, but there was also a proper recognition that Sir John was endeavouring to give us a different Lear, less in the poetic tradition, more urgent in its drive at a realistic presentation of senile folly and its terrible conclusion in madness and in agony. For Philip Hope-Wallace there was in this Lear ' positively luminous pointing of the words, as if sometimes one is really hearing and understanding him for the first time,' and also in the later scenes ' pathos in resignation and humility hard to match.' *The Times* complained that Sir John broke up the verse into prose fragments and in the *Daily Telegraph* W. A. Darlington commented that this great actor had never been so ineffective, and surmised that the decoration and the sound-score ' had got him down. ' But there were some strong appraisals, both here and abroad, of Sir John's fresh drive into the essence of Lear the man. Discussion of this reading of the part, and, more especially of the decoration, deflected notice from the rest of the cast, but Claire Bloom, who played Cordelia in London – Mary Watson took that part on tour in England – was much liked and Milton Shulman of the *Evening Standard*, a critic not easy to satisfy, found her delivery of the lines 'impeccable.' (During the Continental tours Peggy Ashcroft took Cordelia's part, an assurance of high quality.) It was generally thought that the rest of the team were not to be judged as though they were acting in normal circumstances and that Mr. Noguchi had put them under a handicap which made censorious verdicts unfair.

So ended a year of great and various endeavour and experiment, a year in which the sovereign talents of the British theatre had been working for Stratford at Stratford, in English cities and in many of the European capitals. If *King Lear* had surprised by its oddness, *Titus Andronicus* had no less astonished by its victory over intractable material. It was naturally a year which threw a very great strain on the administrative and technical staff and grateful acknowledgements were due to the Stage Directors, Stage Managers, Assistant Stage Managers, and their fellow-craftsmen in both companies. Critical tributes rarely go to the names at the end of the programme, names of unseen persons with a wide range of skills. Their efficiency is vital to the execution of the producer's wishes and so to the safe conduct of any production. Such tributes were fully earned. To carry two Shakespearian productions on a foreign tour with frequent moves and short stays in one capital after another demands the most careful planning and execution : in this staff-work there has been at Stratford a high level of preparation and execution, ranging from the Directors and General Manager through all departments.

For 1956 there was a less ambitious policy. There would be concentration on Stratford, where, in addition to the worthy staging of the plays, there are always domestic problems of finance, internal administration, structural changes, and development of amenities both for players and playgoers.

Emlyn Williams came in to tackle Shylock, Iago, and Angelo, and Harry Andrews returned as King Claudius, Don Armado, and Othello. In the last, his first major tragic role at Stratford, Harry Andrews had a great success. Alan Badel was another to return with big responsibilities; he had to open the season as Hamlet. Diana Churchill was, with Emlyn Williams, a distinguished newcomer. Queen Gertrude and Emilia were her two chief roles. Margaret Johnston was another recruit to Stratford and she quickly bettered expectation as Portia and as Desdemona. That there were no titles in the company this year did not dismay the public: the advance booking was as big as ever.

Hamlet, not seen at Stratford for eight years, came in stark simplicity. Michael Langham's production, with a setting of the most austere kind, arranged by Michael Northen, had no appeal of spectacle. The stage revealed a low dais with a surround of black curtains, broken only by one feature which it baffled the critics to describe. Was it ' a symbolic pillar ' or ' an isolated arras ' ? There was, for the Court, no furniture. Considering that Claudius had risked so much to snatch a throne it was odd that after he had done his deed of darkness, he should have not even a stool to sit upon. (In the play scene he and his queen were at last supplied with this moderate ration of support.) This funereal drapery dispelled any contrast between Hamlet in his suit of woe and the King and courtiers so swiftly and so far removed from mourning. The Prince, instead of being a living protest against the ' heavy-headed revel ' seemed to be moving among the trappings of a general melancholy.

Yet there were advantages. The black background, which was maintained, was, with cleverly directed lighting, an excellent frame for the facial play of the actors. A friend, who often misses points in the theatre owing to shortness of sight, found the play delightfully visible in all the detail of performance. There could, of course, be no delays owing to scenic alterations and the play was accordingly given, with a very full text, at commendable speed. The performance of Alan Badel puzzled the critics and many of the observations passed on it were contradictory. He had rejected romanticism and chose, or allowed his producer to choose for him, a form of clothing which could not have been worn by any actor aiming at a glass-of-fashion manner. Ugly, ill-fitting trousers below a clumsy jacket that made the actor look top-heavy were invariably commented upon with surprise and distaste. (The ' strait strossers ' mentioned derisively in *Henry V* as proper to the ' kerns of Ireland ' had come to royal Denmark.) Still, the apparel need not always proclaim the man and Alan Badel did manage to live down his wardrobe. He is an actor of keen vehemence and he flung himself into the doubts, despairs, and sudden, fiery actions of Hamlet with a full display of feeling and a full flood of eloquence. There was no acting by hint and suggestion in his case : it was performance to the full, even to the point of obvious physical exhaustion in the outpouring of a grief. At a time when there is so much playing down and the finest of Shakespeare's lines may be thrown away, if the producer be one of those who care much for the visual and little for the audible effect, it was a stimulating change to have a Hamlet who thus gripped his part by the throat. It was this fine frenzy of attack which caused the complaints (I think unfair) about a febrile and hysterical Prince. The audience could justly have looked for a less deterrent view of Denmark and its haberdashery: it had no case for deciding that it was not getting the full impact of Shakespeare's powerful creation. One spectator told me that this was to see Hamlet plain, a young man on the rack, and not just an actor with ' a name ' doing something spectacular with a historic role.

Harry Andrews, as the King, won some striking tributes. ' The most complete Claudius we are ever likely to see.' Perhaps it was not more complete than that of Alec Clunes in the otherwise undistinguished production of the play that went to Moscow in the winter of 1955. But here was a handsome rogue with the intelligence necessary to win an intelligent Gertrude. For so Diana Churchill made the Queen, avoiding the usual picture of a soft, silly sensuality. This performance was of the utmost interest, being unusual in its portrait of a hard, scheming woman with her wits about her; it was undervalued in the notices. Dilys Hamlett's Ophelia was questioned on various and inconsistent grounds. It passed with me. Andrew Faulds made a fine Laertes, Mark Dignam was a properly resonant and sepulchral Ghost, and George Howe was once more my ideal Polonius, not too senile, not too foolish and a believable holder of high office.

After *Hamlet* came *The Merchant of Venice*, produced by Margaret Webster without any straining for novelty and decorated by Alan Tagg with a happy return to conventional town and country planning for Venice and Belmont. The first night audience was obviously delighted when the curtain rose on colour in plenty and colour in taste ; the all-black view of Elsinore could be forgotten.

It was generally agreed that the Shylock of Emlyn Williams held an admirable balance between a sympathetic portrait of the hounded Jew and a melodramatic study in vindictive savagery. This maintenance of proportion, in a large theatre, in addition to the actor's small physique and a diction always clear but not notably powerful, meant that this Shylock was not likely to hit an audience with any shattering force. Derek Monsey in *The Sunday Express* hit it off, in my opinion, exactly. ' Excitingly clever: anxiously thought out and nervously carried off. My own bet is that within a month it will be masterly.' The performance, in point of fact, did not need a month to ripen: it was so obviously growing during the first evening. The mixture of venom and pathos in the Trial Scene could hardly be faulted for any lack of compelling veracity even by those who were looking for something more theatrically impressive.

Margaret Johnston proved to be a delightful Portia, with the right youth and gaiety and with an easy, unforced delivery of the lady's wit as well as of her tender feelings. Basil Hoskins won general favour with his handsome Bassanio, as did Anthony Nicholls with Antonio. George Howe made the unusual ' double ' of Old Gobbo and the Duke of Venice and was as credible in the dignity of his dukedom as in his sightless senility. Prunella Scales made a pretty midget of Nerissa but Jeannette Sterke's Jessica was scarcely up to expectation. The setting of Belmont was fascinating and David William gave good utterance to Lorenzo's lines which are so lovely that familiarity can here breed content.

Othello, Stratford's second within three years, brought Harry Andrews to a frontal position which his excellence in supporting parts had long promised and justified. His performance collided with a whole mass-attack of Moors: the ' Old Vic ' had provided two portraits of the General, Television another, Orson Welles a film, and the Soviet film-industry yet another screen version. I cannot pretend to have kept up with all this output, but I can claim to have found in Harry Andrews one of the most credible Othellos of my experience. Here was a soldier of authority and ability who could well have been the hero of Venice and of Desdemona too. It is always a well-nigh impossible task to make believable the swift transition from this martial and marital paragon to the disgusting creature who so lightly swallows such an unlikely story against his wife and then, with maniac bestiality, proclaims that he will chop her into messes. Harry Andrews could not, of course, make us believe in the whole of this improbable and unbearable story, but he brought to the beautiful poetry, in which so much of the ugliness is wrapped, a fine quality of speech and also a livid, lurid show of passionate jealousy. I had previously wondered whether he had this at his command, and I was most glad to have my doubts dispelled.

As Iago Emlyn Williams once more provided a model of clear speech: he patterned the delivery of his lines in a curiously precise way. Delighting in his own devilry, he discoursed of his villainy with perfect clarity without loss of speed. Moreover, he buzzed about his Othello with the right gad-fly tenacity, injecting his poison with neat jabs to the heart. He made a believable ' Ancient ' to attend a believable General; I thought the critics were, in general, less than just to the merits of both these performances.

Desdemona, as a rule, gets a polite, perfunctory last line in the notices. Margaret

Johnston made so striking a figure of the doomed wife that there could be no such dismissal in her case. Desdemona became to us, as indeed she always should, a woman of character who knows her own mind in matrimony, defies the colour-bar with courage, and cannot be wholly dominated when her doom is upon her. Diana Churchill's Emilia had all that fine actress's power to give authenticity to character and emotional power to a line whether it stings a scoundrel or soothes a martyr. The producer in this case was Glen Byam Shaw and, as always in his case, the action ran smoothly and rapidly without any signs of directive exhibitionism. The Motley settings were attractive and workmanlike. It sometimes happens in the theatre that a production is enhanced by something external to what Hamlet called ' the necessary question of the play ': it may even be something fundamentally silly which strikes the fancy of the audience. There are no flukes of this kind in a Byam Shaw production. He works with a plan, with his players, and with the best, if not the showiest, kind of results.

The fourth play of the year was *Love's Labour's Lost*. Peter Hall, a young producer with a reputation rapidly and justly won, had his first Stratford assignment and another newcomer was Geraldine McEwan, who played the Princess of France with a happy, kittenish grace and a pretty sense of the plot's high-spirited artifice. The decoration was in the hands of James Bailey, who displayed his rich command of colour in bringing the Renaissance courtiers on parade.

It is a very difficult piece to handle, since it contains so many topical allusions and so much of the intricate word-play that apparently bewitched the Elizabethans and can be very baffling to us. The opening night was not until July, when the Stratford Theatre begins to be full of American and Continental visitors. This particular specimen of the ' conceited,' sonneteering Tudor style surely needs easing for ears unused to the play's exotic vocabulary and joy in verbal patterns. The text is full of topical allusions as well as of tongue-twisters and might have been cut with advantage, so that the lines could have been less rushed and spoken more clearly. But style of movement and vivacity of comic manoeuvre were abundant and the audience obviously enjoyed all they saw, even if they failed to grasp all that was said.

The scene, in Navarre, is a park with a palace in it. Mr. Bailey rejected the usual boskage of the setting in favour of the building, and some critics resented his offering of a palace with its park left out. But it was handsome architecture and the costumes blazed superbly in this royal Academe of self-denying scholars who, when ladies' eyes rain influence, so soon become more lenient to their starved senses. The part of Berowne fascinates because it seems to conform so closely to Shakespeare's own feelings about love, learning, ' and the huge army of the world's desires.' Alan

Badel gave lively, shrewdly pointed utterance to Berowne's sardonic wit and mockery of his fellows when the oaths are broken. But was he sufficiently heart-struck by the dark lady that is Rosaline? There is the pain of passion as well as the badinage of a courtly flirtation in the wordy warfare of these two. Jeannette Sterke made a mercurial figure of Rosaline, swift in repartee, and the comedy scenes went briskly, despite the comparative quietude of Harry Andrews in the role of the fantastic braggart, Armado. Mark Dignam, not long ago a glorious Holofernes for the 'Old Vic,' improved even on that glory. Clive Revill clowned well as Costard, and Toby Robertson was an admirably innocent Nathaniel.

The company's richness in comedy was again noticeable in *Measure for Measure*. Alan Badel's Lucio was a masterpiece of quick-fire mockery, sharp, cruel, and glittering as a dagger. Among the clowns Patrick Wymark excelled as Pompey and John Garley as Elbow. Diana Churchill's Mistress Overdone would have been immense if Shakespeare had not seemed to forget that shameless faggot and so had left the part underdone. Ron Haddrick and Clive Revill added amply to the fantastic fooling in the jaws of death.

Anthony Quayle's production showed a vigorous belief in a play disliked by many. He seized the preposterous plot and forced it to seem credible, in which feat he had admirable assistance from Anthony Nicholls as the Duke. It is a short play and need not be hustled; the speaking of the lines showed Stratford, not always strong and clear in this, at its best.

Incidentally, Escalus and the Provost, who sometimes seem shadowy, emerged as real persons; George Howe and Mark Dignam supplied this striking authenticity. Margaret Johnston was again, and justly, acclaimed for the compelling sincerity of her Isabella, while Emlyn Williams brought to Angelo a memorable essay in tight-lipped and odious hypocrisy. Angelo is a part in which concealed and burning emotion has to be conveyed with the utmost economy of expression; that tortured restraint was most cleverly achieved.

Mr. Quayle had to stand comparison with a brilliant production by Peter Brook six years ago, a point on which criticism picked. He went his own way, very properly, and did not try to repeat another man's effects; his own were effective, although the scene (by Tanya Moiseiwitsch) seemed to some excessively dark and sometimes under-lit. But there could be no doubt of the public approbation, and as has been said, the comedy was exceptionally entertaining. It was sad news that this was Anthony Quayle's last production as a Director of the Theatre. He came to Stratford as an actor in 1948 and was appointed Director in the same year, since when his work in administration as well as in production and performance has been arduous and immensely successful. A man of his varied talents naturally needs larger scope after so many years in office, and Stratford's loss will be London's gain; so Glen Byam Shaw, his colleague, can take over with the confidence and good wishes of all.

It was good news that Fordham Flower received a knighthood for his excellent work as Chairman of the Council of the Shakespeare Memorial Theatre during the post-war years of change and expansion. He has notably added, with his energy and judgment, to his family's long service of Shakespeare and of Stratford, and the honour was as popular as it was merited.

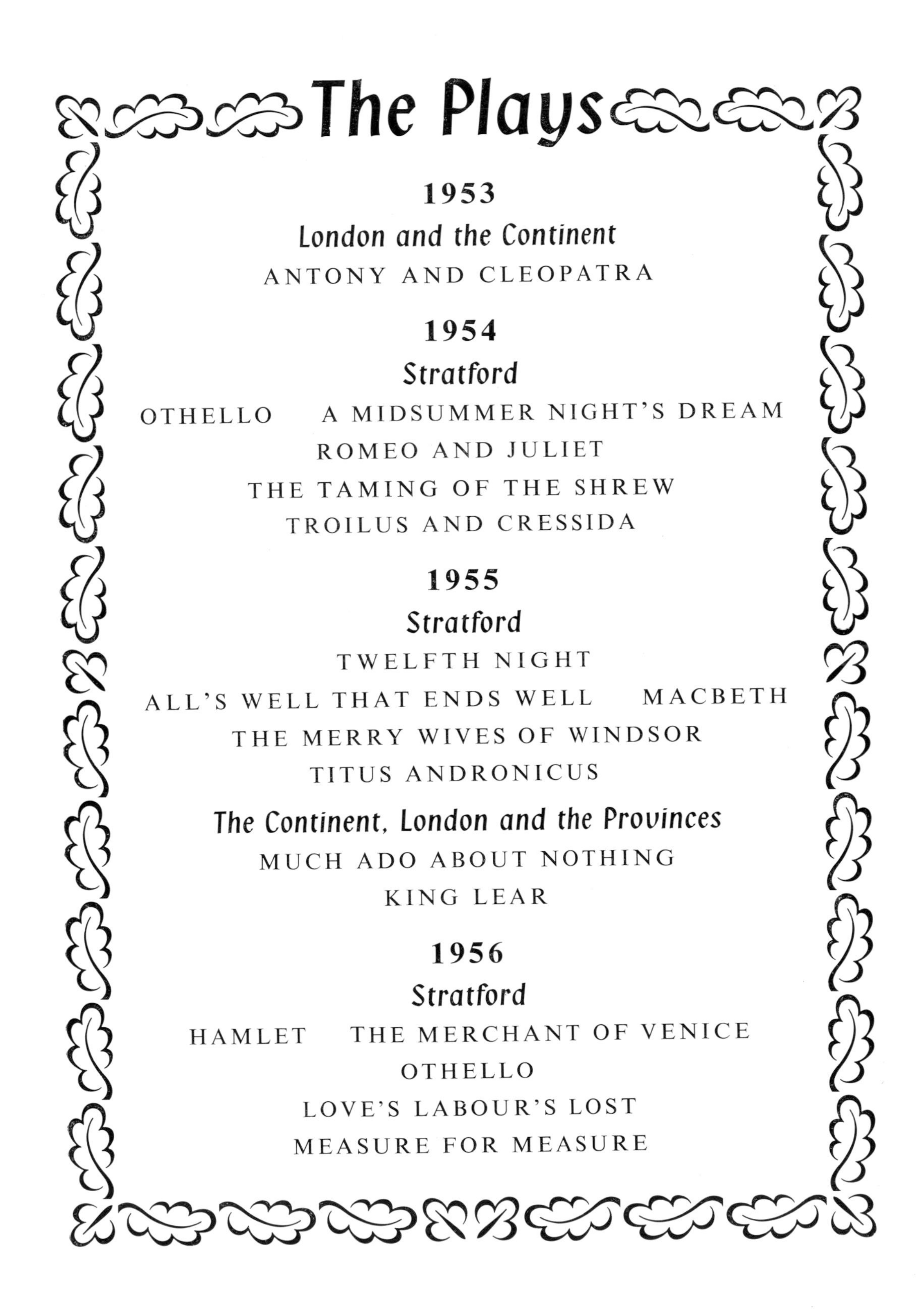

The Plays

1953

London and the Continent

ANTONY AND CLEOPATRA

1954

Stratford

OTHELLO   A MIDSUMMER NIGHT'S DREAM

ROMEO AND JULIET

THE TAMING OF THE SHREW

TROILUS AND CRESSIDA

1955

Stratford

TWELFTH NIGHT

ALL'S WELL THAT ENDS WELL   MACBETH

THE MERRY WIVES OF WINDSOR

TITUS ANDRONICUS

The Continent, London and the Provinces

MUCH ADO ABOUT NOTHING

KING LEAR

1956

Stratford

HAMLET   THE MERCHANT OF VENICE

OTHELLO

LOVE'S LABOUR'S LOST

MEASURE FOR MEASURE

Antony and Cleopatra

LONDON AND THE CONTINENT NOVEMBER 1953 TO JANUARY 1954

ANTONY ...	Triumvirs	MICHAEL REDGRAVE
OCTAVIUS CÆSAR	Triumvirs	MARIUS GORING
LEPIDUS ...	Triumvirs	DONALD PLEASENCE
SEXTUS POMPEIUS		TONY BRITTON
MENAS, *friend to Pompeius* ...		MICHAEL WARRE
PHILO	*Friends to Antony and Officers of his forces*	MICHAEL TURNER
DOMITIUS ENOBARBUS	*Friends to Antony and Officers of his forces*	HARRY ANDREWS
VENTIDIUS ...	*Friends to Antony and Officers of his forces*	MICHAEL HAYES
CANIDIUS	*Friends to Antony and Officers of his forces*	PHILIP MORANT
SCARUS	*Friends to Antony and Officers of his forces*	JEROME WILLIS
EROS	*Friends to Antony and Officers of his forces*	DAVID O'BRIEN
DERCETAS... ...	*Friends to Antony and Officers of his forces*	PETER DUGUID
OLD SOLDIER *in Antony's Army*		GEORGE HART
A MESSENGER *from Sicyon* ...		PETER NORRIS
DEMETRIUS ...		BERNARD KAY
THIDIAS	*Friends to Cæsar and Officers of his forces*	WILLIAM PEACOCK
MÆCENAS ...	*Friends to Cæsar and Officers of his forces*	DONALD ECCLES
AGRIPPA	*Friends to Cæsar and Officers of his forces*	JOHN BUSHELLE
TAURUS	*Friends to Cæsar and Officers of his forces*	BERNARD KAY
DOLABELLA ...	*Friends to Cæsar and Officers of his forces*	ROBERT SHAW
GALLUS	*Friends to Cæsar and Officers of his forces*	DENYS GRAHAM
PROCULEIUS ...	*Friends to Cæsar and Officers of his forces*	POWYS THOMAS
ALEXAS	*Subjects to Cleopatra*	ALAN TOWNSEND
MARDIAN, *a Eunuch*	*Subjects to Cleopatra*	MERVYN BLAKE
DIOMEDES ...	*Subjects to Cleopatra*	DONALD PLEASENCE
A SOOTHSAYER ...	*Subjects to Cleopatra*	PHILIP MORANT
EUPHRONIUS *a Schoolmaster*	*Subjects to Cleopatra*	PETER NORRIS
SELEUCUS, *a Treasurer*	*Subjects to Cleopatra*	GARETH JONES
A MESSENGER ...	*Subjects to Cleopatra*	POWYS THOMAS
A CLOWN	*Subjects to Cleopatra*	JAMES WELLMAN
A ROMAN SOLDIER		ALAN TOWNSEND
CLEOPATRA, *Queen of Egypt* ...		PEGGY ASHCROFT
OCTAVIA, *Sister to Cæsar* ...		RACHEL KEMPSON
CHARMIAN	*Attendants on Cleopatra*	JEAN WILSON
IRAS ...	*Attendants on Cleopatra*	MARY WATSON

Soldiers, Attendants and Slaves:
DIANA CHADWICK, MARIGOLD CHARLESWORTH, ANTHONY ADAMS, DENNIS CLINTON, JAMES CULLIFORD, NIGEL DAVENPORT, JOHN GLENDENNING, CHARLES GRAY, RALPH HALLETT, CHARLES HOWARD, PETER JOHNSON, DAVID KING, RICHARD MARTIN, JOHN ROBERTS, RAYMOND SHERRY.

The Play directed by GLEN BYAM SHAW
Scenery and Costumes designed by MOTLEY *Music by* ANTONY HOPKINS
Dance arranged by PAULINE GRANT *Lighting by* PETER STREULI

Rachel Kempson as Octavia

IRAS (*Act IV Scene 15*) Royal Egypt, Empress!

Opposite
ANTONY (*Act I Scene I*) The nobleness of life Is to do thus . . .

CLEOPATRA (*Act I Scene 1*) *Above*
If it be love indeed, tell me how much

CAESAR (*Act IV Scene 1*) *Below*
He calls me boy, and chides as he had power
To beat me out of Egypt

FIRST SOLDIER (*Act IV Scene 10*) *Opposite*
The hand of death has raught him

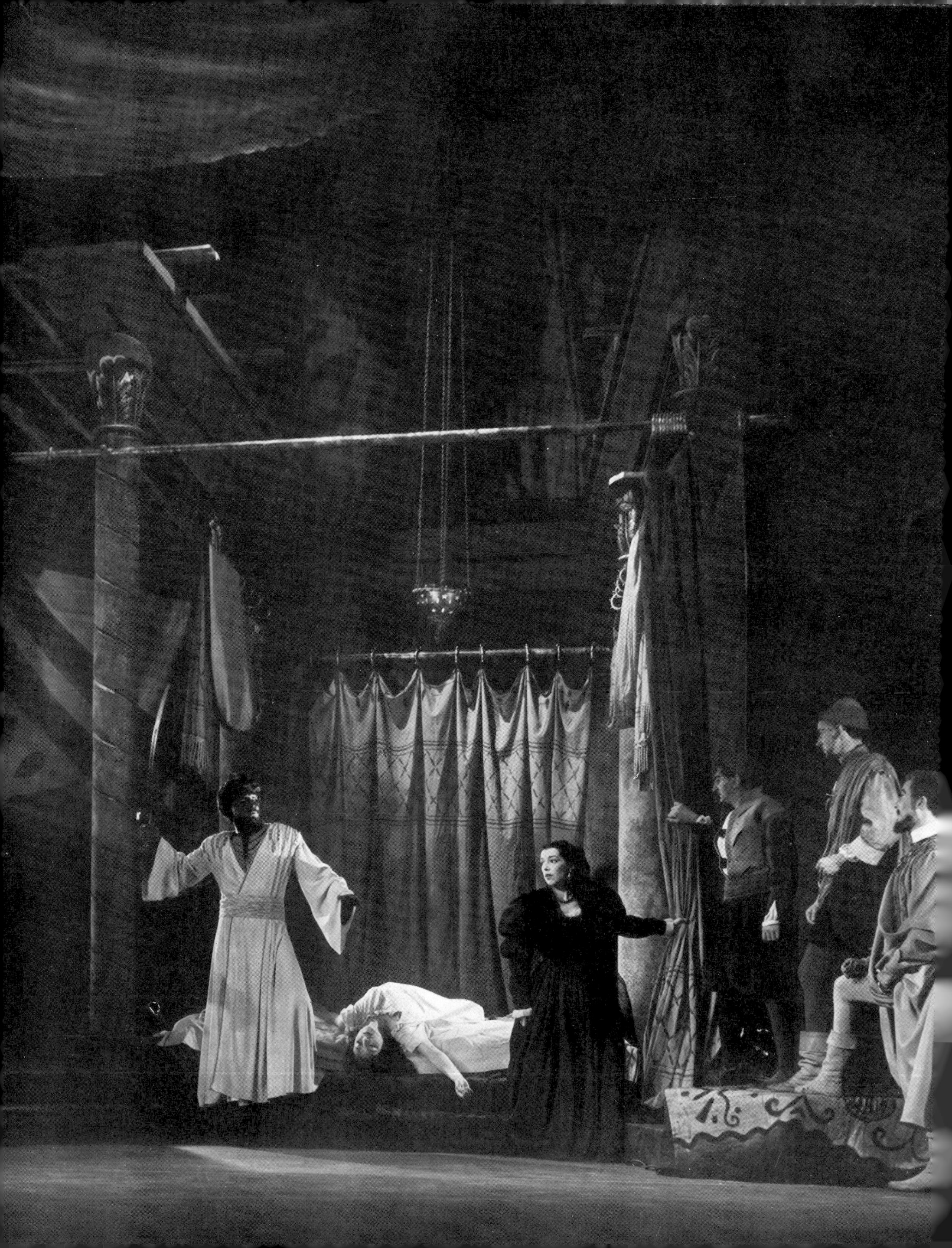

Othello

1954 SEASON

RODERIGO	POWYS THOMAS
IAGO	RAYMOND WESTWELL
BRABANTIO	WILLIAM DEVLIN
OTHELLO	ANTHONY QUAYLE
CASSIO	TONY BRITTON
SENATORS {	IAN MULLINS
... ...	EDWARD ATIENZA
THE DUKE OF VENICE ...	PHILIP MORANT
LODOVICO...	BASIL HOSKINS
GRATIANO	MERVYN BLAKE
FIRST MESSENGER	RAYMOND SHERRY
SECOND MESSENGER ...	FRANK WATERS
DESDEMONA	BARBARA JEFFORD
MONTANO...	BERNARD KAY
OFFICERS AT CYPRUS { ...	GEORGE HART
...	JEROME WILLIS
...	IAN BANNEN
EMILIA	JOAN MACARTHUR
HERALD	... DAVID KING
BIANCA	MURIEL PAVLOW

Senators, Servants and Soldiers:
JILL CARY, JEAN MORLEY, GEOFFREY ADAMS, PHILIP ANTONY, RICHARD COE, BEVERLEY CROSS, PETER DUGUID, RON HADDRICK, IAN HOLM, KEVIN MILES, TIMOTHY PARKES, DONALD PICKERING, JAMES VILLIERS

The Play directed by ANTHONY QUAYLE *assisted by* PATRICK DONNELL
Scenery and Costumes designed by TANYA MOISEIWITSCH *Music composed by* LESLIE BRIDGEWATER
Fights arranged by PATRICK CREAN *Lighting by* JULIA WOOTTEN

IAGO (*Act III Scene 3*)
O, beware, my lord, of jealousy

EMILIA (*Act V Scene 2*) *Opposite*
Do thy worst:
This deed of thine is no more worthy heaven
Than thou wast worthy her

OTHELLO (*Act IV Scene 1*)
It gives me wonder great as my content
To see you here before me

Opposite
Tony Britton as Cassio and Muriel Pavlow as Bianca

A Midsummer Night's Dream

1954 SEASON

THESEUS, *Duke of Athens* ...	KEITH MICHELL
HIPPOLYTA, *Queen of the Amazons* ...	JEAN WILSON
PHILOSTRATE, *Master of the Revels*	EDWARD ATIENZA
EGEUS, *Father to Hermia*	GEOFFREY BAYLDON
HERMIA	ZENA WALKER
DEMETRIUS	BASIL HOSKINS
LYSANDER	TONY BRITTON
HELENA	BARBARA JEFFORD
QUINCE, *a carpenter*	LEO McKERN
BOTTOM, *a weaver*	ANTHONY QUAYLE
FLUTE, *a bellows-mender*	IAN BANNEN
STARVELING, *a tailor*	PETER DUGUID
SNOUT, *a tinker*	JAMES GROUT
SNUG, *a joiner*	MERVYN BLAKE
PUCK, *or Robin Goodfellow* ...	DAVID O'BRIEN
A FAIRY	JEAN MORLEY
OBERON, *King of the Fairies* ...	POWYS THOMAS
TITANIA, *Queen of the Fairies* ...	MURIEL PAVLOW
PEASEBLOSSOM (*Fairies*) ...	ANNETTE APCAR (*From 4th August* DOONE BINGEMAN)
COBWEB (*Fairies*) ...	AUDREY SEED
MOTH (*Fairies*)	JILL CARY
MUSTARDSEED (*Fairies*) ...	ALEXANDRA JACK

Attendants on Theseus, Hippolyta and Oberon:
JAN BASHFORD, BEVERLEY CROSS, DAVID KING, KEVIN MILES, TIMOTHY PARKES, DONALD PICKERING, JOHN TURNER, JAMES VILLIERS, FRANK WATERS.

The Play directed by GEORGE DEVINE
Scenery and Costumes designed by MOTLEY *Music composed by* ROBERTO GERHARD
Choreography by PAULINE GRANT *Lighting by* PETER STREULI

THISBE (*Act V Scene 1*)
Asleep my love? What, dead my dove?

Jean Wilson as Hippolyta and Keith Michell as Theseus

Opposite
Muriel Pavlow as Titania and Powys Thomas as Oberon

SNOUT (*Act III Scene 1*) *Above*
Doth the moon shine,
that night we play our play?

DEMETRIUS (*Act III Scene 2*) *Below*
O, let me kiss
This princess of pure white, this seal of bliss!

Opposite
David O'Brien as Puck

Romeo and Juliet

1954 SEASON

CHORUS	JAMES GROUT
SAMPSON (Servants to Capulet)	MERVYN BLAKE
GREGORY (Servants to Capulet)	BERNARD KAY
PETER (Servants to Capulet)	GEOFFREY BAYLDON
ANTHONY (Servants to Capulet)	IAN BANNEN
POTPAN (Servants to Capulet)	DAVID KING
OLD MAN (Servants to Capulet)	GEORGE HART
ABRAHAM (Servants to Montague)	JOHN TURNER
BALTHASAR (Servants to Montague)	JEROME WILLIS
TYBALT, *Nephew to Lady Capulet*	KEITH MICHELL
TYBALT'S PAGE	DAVID O'BRIEN
BENVOLIO, *Nephew to Montague*	POWYS THOMAS
CAPULET	WILLIAM DEVLIN
LADY CAPULET	JEAN WILSON
MONTAGUE	PHILIP MORANT
LADY MONTAGUE	JOAN MACARTHUR
PRINCE OF VERONA	RAYMOND WESTWELL
ROMEO	LAURENCE HARVEY
PARIS, *Kinsman to the Prince*	DONALD PICKERING
PARIS'S PAGE	IAN HOLM
JULIET	ZENA WALKER
NURSE, *to Juliet*	ROSALIND ATKINSON
MERCUTIO	TONY BRITTON
MERCUTIO'S PAGE	RAYMOND SHERRY
COUSIN CAPULET	IAN MULLINS
FRIAR LAURENCE	LEO MCKERN
AN APOTHECARY	PETER DUGUID
FRIAR JOHN	EDWARD ATIENZA
FIRST WATCH	JAMES GROUT

Citizens of Verona and Mantua, Kinsfolk of both Houses, Guards, Watchmen, Musicians and Servants:

ANNETTE APCAR, JAN BASHFORD, JILL CARY, JANE HOLLAND, JEAN MORLEY, AUDREY SEED, GEOFFREY ADAMS, PHILIP ANTHONY, RICHARD COE, BEVERLEY CROSS, RON HADDRICK, KEVIN MILES, TIMOTHY PARKES, FRANK WATERS, JAMES VILLIERS.

The Play directed by GLEN BYAM SHAW
Scenery and Costumes designed by MOTLEY *Music composed by* ANTONY HOPKINS *Dance arranged by* PAULINE GRANT
Fights arranged by BERNARD HEPTON & JOHN GREENWOOD *Lighting by* PETER STREULI

Tony Britton as Mercutio

Rosalind Atkinson as the Nurse

ROMEO (*Act II Scene 2*) *Opposite*
How silver sweet sound lovers' tongues by night, Like softest music to attending ears

BENVOLIO (*Act II Scene 6*) *Opposite*
Stand not amaz'd, the Prince will doom thee death
If thou art taken, hence be gone away

FRIAR LAURENCE (*Act IV Scene 5*) *Above*
Peace ho for shame, confusion's cave lives not
In these confusions

Below
Laurence Harvey as Romeo
and Zena Walker as Juliet

The Taming of the Shrew

1954 SEASON

CHRISTOPHER SLY, *a Tinker* ...		JAMES GROUT
HOSTESS *of an ale-house* ...		ROSALIND ATKINSON
A LORD		WILLIAM DEVLIN
HUNTSMEN		FRANK WATERS
		JEROME WILLIS
A PAGE		DONALD PICKERING
THE LORD'S SERVANTS		TIMOTHY PARKES
		RAYMOND SHERRY
		JAMES VILLIERS
THE LORD'S MUSICIANS		DAVID KING
		RICHARD COE
		PHILIP ANTHONY

Players, impersonating

LUCENTIO, *a young Gentleman of Pisa*		BASIL HOSKINS
TRANIO, *his Servant*		JOHN TURNER
BAPTISTA, *a rich Gentleman of Padua*		RAYMOND WESTWELL
KATHARINA, *the Shrew*	*His Daughters*	BARBARA JEFFORD
BIANCA	*His Daughters*	MURIEL PAVLOW
GREMIO ...	*Suitors to Bianca*	EDWARD ATIENZA
HORTENSIO	*Suitors to Bianca*	GEOFFREY BAYLDON
BIONDELLO, *Servant to Lucentio*		DAVID O'BRIEN
PETRUCHIO, *a Gentleman of Verona*		KEITH MICHELL
GRUMIO, *his Servant*		LEO MCKERN
CURTIS	*Servants at Petruchio's country house*	... IAN BANNEN
PETER	*Servants at Petruchio's country house*	GEOFFREY ADAMS
PHILLIP	*Servants at Petruchio's country house*	RON HADDRICK
NATHANIEL	*Servants at Petruchio's country house*	KEVIN MILES
GREGORY	*Servants at Petruchio's country house*	BEVERLEY CROSS
A TAILOR		... IAN MULLINS
A HABERDASHER		GEORGE HART
A PEDANT, *travelling from Mantua*		PETER DUGUID
VINCENTIO, *Father to Lucentio*		PHILIP MORANT
A WIDOW		JEAN WILSON

The Play directed by GEORGE DEVINE

Scenery and Costumes designed by VIVIENNE KERNOT *Music composed by* ROBERTO GERHARD

Lighting by DESMOND HALL

Leo McKern as Grumio and Barbara Jefford as Katharina

PETRUCHIO (*Act III Scene 2*) *Opposite*
She is my goods, my chattels, she is my house
My household stuff, my field, my barn,
My horse, my ox, my ass, my any thing

Left
Rosalind Atkinson as the Hostess

PETRUCHIO (*Act IV Scene 1*) *Opposite*
. . . better 'twere that both of us did fast,
Since of ourselves, ourselves are choleric

Below
Peter Duguid as Vincentio

KATE (*Act II Scene 1*) *Opposite*
Of all thy suitors here I charge thee tell
Whom thou lov'st best: see thou dissemble not

CHRISTOPHER SLY (*Induction Scene 2*) *Above*
For God's sake a pot of small ale

KATE (*Act V Scene 2*) *Below*
Fie, fie, unknit that threatening unkind brow

Troilus and Cressida

1954 SEASON

PROLOGUE	... ...	James Grout
PRIAM, *King of Troy*	...	Geoffrey Bayldon
HECUBA, *his Queen*	...	Rosalind Atkinson
HECTOR ...	*Priam's Sons*	Raymond Westwell
PARIS ...	*Priam's Sons* ...	Basil Hoskins
HELENUS	*Priam's Sons* ...	David King
DEIPHOBUS	*Priam's Sons* ...	Timothy Parkes
TROILUS ...	*Priam's Sons* ...	Laurence Harvey
CASSANDRA, *Priam's Daughter*		Jean Wilson
ANDROMACHE, *wife to Hector*		Jan Bashford
MARGARELON, *bastard son of Priam*		John Turner
AENEAS	*Trojan Commanders* ...	Powys Thomas
ANTENOR	*Trojan Commanders* ...	Ian Mullins
ALEXANDER, *servant in the Royal Household*	...	Peter Duguid
SERVANT *to Paris*...	... ...	David O'Brien
SERVANT *to Troilus*	... ...	Ian Holm
PANDARUS, *uncle to Cressida*	...	Anthony Quayle
CRESSIDA ...	... ...	Muriel Pavlow
CALCHAS, *her father*	... ...	Edward Atienza
HELEN, *wife to Menelaus*	...	Barbara Jefford
AGAMEMNON, *the Grecian General*		William Devlin
MENELAUS, *his brother* ...	...	Philip Morant
NESTOR ...	*Grecian Commanders* ...	Mervyn Blake
ULYSSES ...	*Grecian Commanders* ...	Leo McKern
AJAX ...	*Grecian Commanders* ...	James Grout
ACHILLES	*Grecian Commanders* ...	Keith Michell
PATROCLUS	*Grecian Commanders* ...	Jerome Willis
DIOMEDES	*Grecian Commanders*	Bernard Kay
THERSITES	... ...	Tony Britton
TRUMPETER *to Ajax*	... ...	Stanley Wheeler

Princes, Soldiers, Servants and Attendants:

Wendy Aitken, Jill Cary, Jane Holland, Jean Morley, Geoffrey Adams, Philip Anthony, Ian Bannen, Richard Coe, Beverley Cross, Ron Haddrick, George Hart, Kevin Miles, Raymond Sherry, Donald Pickering, James Villiers, Frank Waters.

The Play directed by GLEN BYAM SHAW
Scenery and Costumes designed by MALCOLM PRIDE
Music composed by ANTONY HOPKINS
Fights arranged by BERNARD HEPTON & JOHN GREENWOOD
Lighting by PETER STREULI

Right
Laurence Harvey as Troilus

Opposite
Muriel Pavlow as Cressida and Anthony Quayle as Pandarus

AENEAS (*Act I Scene 3*)
We have, great Agamemnon, here in Troy
A prince call'd Hector

Opposite
Basil Hoskins as Paris and Barbara Jefford as Helen

THERSITES (*Act V Scene 4*)
Now they are clapper-clawing one another

ULYSSES (*Act III Scene 3*) *Opposite above*
Time hath, my lord, a wallet at his back . . .

(*Act IV Scene 5*) *Opposite below*
The fight between Hector (*Raymond Westwell*)
and Ajax (*James Grout*)

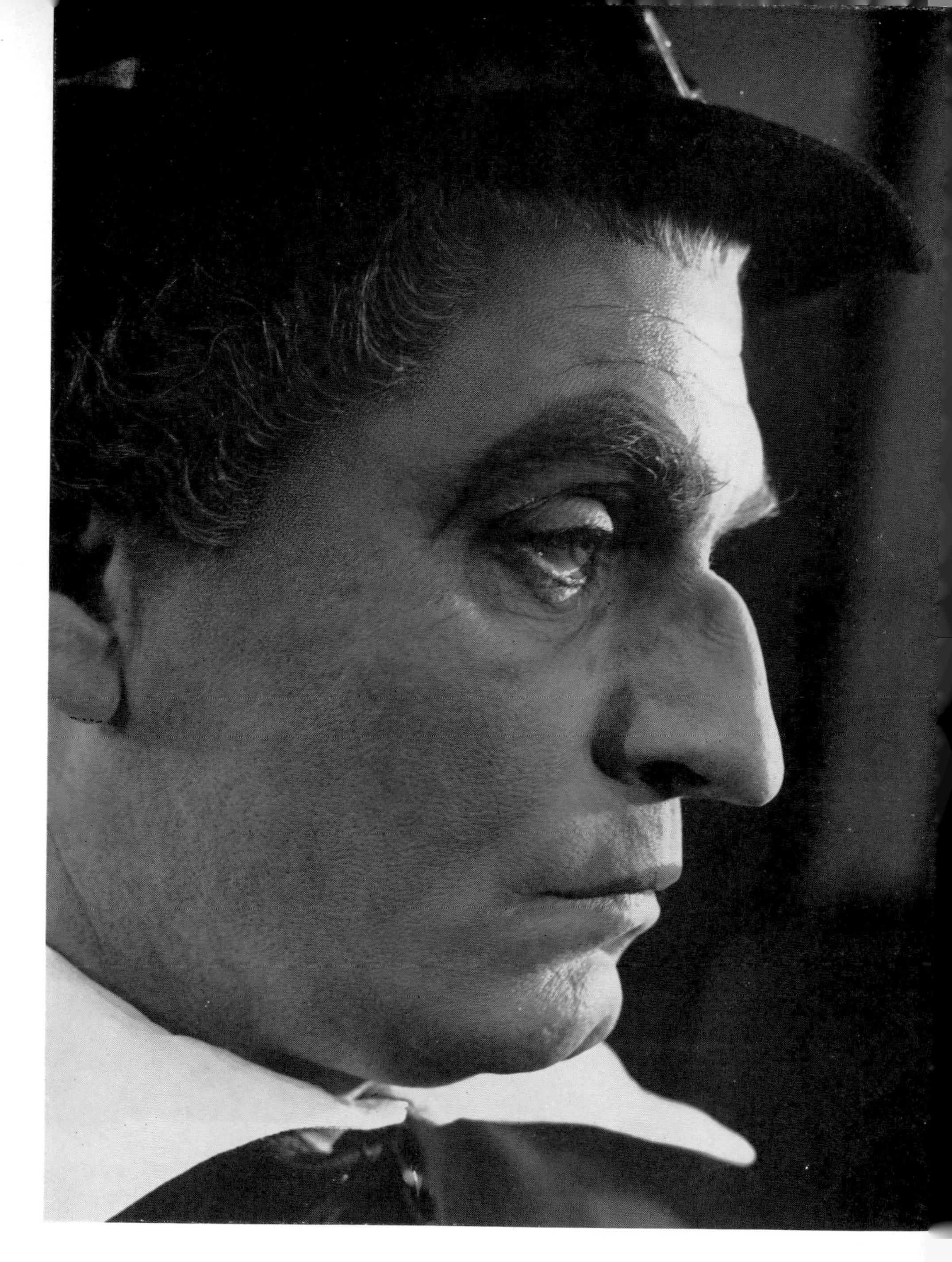

Laurence Olivier as Malvolio

Twelfth Night

1955 SEASON

The Play directed by JOHN GIELGUD
Scenery and Costumes designed by MALCOLM PRIDE
Music by LESLIE BRIDGEWATER
Fights arranged by BERNARD HEPTON & JOHN GREENWOOD
Lighting by PETER STREULI

Vivien Leigh as Viola

ORSINO, *Duke of Illyria*		KEITH MICHELL
CURIO	*Gentlemen attending on the Duke*	RICHARD COE
VALENTINE		GABRIEL WOOLF
VIOLA		... VIVIEN LEIGH
A SEA CAPTAIN		MERVYN BLAKE
SIR TOBY BELCH, *uncle to Olivia*		... ALAN WEBB
MARIA, *Olivia's woman* ...		ANGELA BADDELEY
SIR ANDREW AGUECHEEK ...		MICHAEL DENISON
FESTE, *a Clown*		EDWARD ATIENZA
OLIVIA		MAXINE AUDLEY
MALVOLIO, *her Steward* ...		LAURENCE OLIVIER
FABIAN, *servant to Olivia* ...		LEE MONTAGUE

ANTONIO, *a sea captain, friend to Sebastian*	WILLIAM DEVLIN
SEBASTIAN	TRADER FAULKNER
SERVANT TO OLIVIA	GEORGE LITTLE
OFFICERS	HUGH CROSS JOHN SPRINGETT
PRIEST	PATRICK WYMARK

Attendants, Lords, Sailors and Musicians:
DILYS HAMLETT, MARY LAW, ROBERT ARNOLD, LEON EAGLES, PETER VAN GREENAWAY, ALAN HAYWOOD, IAN HOLM, ROBERT HUNTER, EMRYS JAMES, JOHN MACGREGOR, REX ROBINSON, JOHN SOUTHWORTH, PAUL VIEYRA, GEOFFREY SASSÉ.

ORSINO (*Act I Scene 1*) *Above*
How now, what news from her?

VIOLA (*Act I Scene 2*) *Below*
For saying so, there's gold

OLIVIA (*Act III Scene 2*) *Opposite*
Stay: I prithee, tell me what thou think'st of me

FESTE (*Act V Scene I*)
But that's all one, our play is done,
And we'll strive to please you every day

MALVOLIO (*Act II Scene 5*) *Opposite*
By my life, this is my lady's hand: these be her
very c's, her u's, and her t's

All's Well that Ends Well

1955 SEASON

BERTRAM, *the Count of Rousillon* ... MICHAEL DENISON
COUNTESS OF ROUSILLON, *his Mother* ... ROSALIND ATKINSON
LAFEU ... RALPH MICHAEL
HELENA, *a waiting gentlewoman to the Countess* ... JOYCE REDMAN
PAROLLES ... KEITH MICHELL
A PAGE, *serving Bertram* ... IAN HOLM
THE KING OF FRANCE ... ALAN WEBB
CHAMBERLAINS ... MERVYN BLAKE, DAVID KING
RINALDO, *Steward to the Countess* ... GEOFFREY BAYLDON
LAVACHE, *Clown to the Countess* ... EDWARD ATIENZA
CAPT. DUMAIN, HIS BROTHER, *Gentlemen at the French Court* ... HUGH CROSS, PATRICK WYMARK
COURTIERS ... TRADER FAULKNER, RICHARD COE, KEVIN MILES, REX ROBINSON
COURIERS ... JAMES GROUT, RON HADDRICK
A WIDOW OF FLORENCE ... NANCYE STEWART
DIANA, *her daughter* ... JILL DIXON
MARIANA, *neighbour to the Widow* ... DILYS HAMLETT
MORGAN, *a Soldier* ... LEE MONTAGUE
A GENTLE ASTRINGER ... JOHN MACGREGOR

Ladies in Waiting, Lords, Officers, Priests, Soldiers, Citizens, and Attendants:

ANN FIRBANK, MARY LAW, ROBERT ARNOLD, LEON EAGLES, PETER VAN GREENAWAY, ALAN HAYWOOD, ROBERT HUNTER, EMRYS JAMES, GEORGE LITTLE, GEOFFREY SASSÉ, JOHN SOUTHWORTH, JOHN SPRINGETT, PAUL VIEYRA, GABRIEL WOOLF.

The Play directed by NOEL WILLMAN
Scenery and Costumes designed by MARIANO ANDREU *Music composed by* ANTONY HOPKINS
Dance movements arranged by GERDA RINK *Lighting by* PETER STREULI *Technical Adviser* MICHAEL NORTHEN

Edward Atienza as Lavache

Jill Dixon as Diana

HELENA (*Act II Scene 1*) *Opposite*
Then shalt thou give me with thy kingly hand
What husband in thy power I will command

THE KING (*Act II Scene 3*) *Above*
Peruse them well:
Not one of those but had a noble father

PAROLLES (*Act II Scene 3*) *Below*
Nay, 'tis strange, 'tis very strange, that is the brief and the tedious of it, and he's of a most facinerious spirit . . .

Opposite
Rosalind Atkinson as the Countess of Rousillon and Joyce Redman as Helena

Macbeth

1955 SEASON

THE WEIRD SISTERS ...	DILYS HAMLETT NANCYE STEWART MARY LAW
DUNCAN, *King of Scotland*	GEOFFREY BAYLDON
MALCOLM } *Duncan's*	TRADER FAULKNER
DONALBAIN } *sons*	... IAN HOLM
A SERGEANT	... DAVID KING
ROSS	WILLIAM DEVLIN
LENNOX	JAMES GROUT
ANGUS	JOHN SPRINGETT
MENTEITH	ROBERT HUNTER
CAITHNESS	GABRIEL WOOLF
MACBETH	LAURENCE OLIVIER
BANQUO	RALPH MICHAEL
FLEANCE, *Banquo's son* ...	... PAUL VIEYRA
LADY MACBETH	... VIVIEN LEIGH
SEYTON	LEE MONTAGUE
A PORTER	PATRICK WYMARK
AN OLD MAN	JOHN MACGREGOR
TWO MURDERERS ...	RON HADDRICK HUGH CROSS
MACDUFF	KEITH MICHELL
LADY MACDUFF	MAXINE AUDLEY
MACDUFF'S SON ...	... JOHN ROGERS
A SHEPHERD	MERVYN BLAKE
A DOCTOR	GEOFFREY BAYLDON
A GENTLEWOMAN	ROSALIND ATKINSON
A SERVANT	...RICHARD COE
SIWARD *general of the English forces*	MERVYN BLAKE
SIWARD'S SON	ROBERT ARNOLD
A SENTRY	REX ROBINSON

Lords, Soldiers, Attendants and others:
JILL DIXON, ANN FIRBANK, LEON EAGLES, PETER VAN GREENAWAY, ALAN HAYWOOD, EMRYS JAMES, GEORGE LITTLE, KEVIN MILES, GEOFFREY SASSÉ, JOHN SOUTHWORTH, PHILIP THOMAS.

The Play directed by GLEN BYAM SHAW
Scenery and Costumes designed by ROGER FURSE
Music by ANTONY HOPKINS
Fights arranged by
BERNARD HEPTON & JOHN GREENWOOD
Lighting by PETER STREULI

Vivien Leigh as Lady Macbeth

Opposite
Keith Michell as Macduff and Laurence Olivier as Macbeth

DUNCAN (*Act I Scene 6*)
See, see, our honour'd hostess!

FIRST WITCH (*Act I Scene 1*) *Opposite*
When shall we three meet again?
In thunder, lightning, or in rain?

Maxine Audley as Lady Macduff

Ralph Michael as Banquo

Opposite
LADY MACBETH (*Act V Scene I*)
What, will these hands ne'er be clean?

Patrick Wymark as the Porter

William Devlin as Ross

MACDUFF (*Act V Scene 8*)
Hail, King of Scotland!

Opposite
Laurence Olivier as Macbeth

The Merry Wives of Windsor

1955 SEASON

JUSTICE SHALLOW	EDWARD ATIENZA
ABRAHAM SLENDER, *his cousin*	GEOFFREY BAYLDON
SIR HUGH EVANS, *a School Master*	WILLIAM DEVLIN
MASTER PAGE	RALPH MICHAEL
MISTRESS PAGE	ANGELA BADDELEY
ANNE, *their daughter*	JILL DIXON
WILLIAM, *their son*	PHILIP THOMAS
MASTER FORD	KEITH MICHELL
MISTRESS FORD	JOYCE REDMAN
SIR JOHN FALSTAFF	ANTHONY QUAYLE
BARDOLPH (*his followers*) ...	ROBERT HUNTER
PISTOL (*his followers*)	JAMES GROUT
NYM (*his followers*) ...	MERVYN BLAKE
ROBIN (*his followers*)	JOHN ROGERS
THE HOST OF THE GARTER INN	PATRICK WYMARK
DOCTOR CAIUS	MICHAEL DENISON
MISTRESS QUICKLY, *his nurse*	ROSALIND ATKINSON
FENTON	TRADER FAULKNER
SIMPLE, *servant to Slender* ...	GEOFFREY SASSÉ
RUGBY, *servant to Dr Caius* ...	JOHN SOUTHWORTH
JOHN (*servants to Mistress Ford*) ...	REX ROBINSON
ROBERT (*servants to Mistress Ford*) ...	ALAN HAYWOOD

A Bear Trainer, A Bear, A Constable, Townsfolk, Boys and Servants:

ANN FIRBANK, MARY LAW, NANCYE STEWART, HUGH CROSS, LEON EAGLES, RON HADDRICK, IAN HOLM, JOHN MACGREGOR, KEVIN MILES, DAVID TILLEY.

The Play directed by GLEN BYAM SHAW
Scenery and Costumes designed by MOTLEY *Music by* LESLIE BRIDGEWATER
Dances arranged by PAULINE GRANT *Lighting by* PETER STREULI

Michael Denison as Doctor Caius

Rosalind Atkinson as Mistress Quickly

Opposite
Falstaff hides in the buck-basket so as not to be seen by Mistress Ford's husband (Act III Scene 3)

FALSTAFF (*Act I Scene 1*) *Opposite above*
Mistress Ford, by my troth you are very well met

FALSTAFF (*Act V Scene 5*) *Opposite below*
Heavens defend me from that Welsh fairy, lest he transform me to a piece of cheese!

FALSTAFF (*Act III Scene 5*)
. . . they convey'd me into a buck-basket
FORD
A buck-basket?
FALSTAFF
By the Lord, a buck-basket!

HOST (*Act III Scene 1*)
Peace, I say! hear mine host of the Garter

Opposite
Joyce Redman as Mistress Ford and Angela Baddeley as Mistress Page

Titus Andronicus

1955 SEASON

SATURNINUS ... ... FRANK THRING
son to the late Emperor of Rome
BASSIANUS, *his brother* ... ... RALPH MICHAEL
MARCUS ANDRONICUS ... ... ALAN WEBB
tribune of the people and brother to Titus
A ROMAN CAPTAIN ... ...JAMES GROUT
TITUS ANDRONICUS ... LAURENCE OLIVIER
LUCIUS ... (*his sons*) ... MICHAEL DENISON
QUINTUS ... (*his sons*) ... LEON EAGLES
MARTIUS ... (*his sons*) ... JOHN MACGREGOR
MUTIUS ... (*his sons*) ... ... IAN HOLM
TAMORA, *Queen of the Goths* ... MAXINE AUDLEY
ALARBUS ... (*her sons*) ... ROBERT ARNOLD
CHIRON ... (*her sons*) ... KEVIN MILES
DEMETRIUS (*her sons*) ... LEE MONTAGUE
AARON, *a Moor* ... ... ANTHONY QUAYLE
LAVINIA, *daughter to Titus Andronicus* VIVIEN LEIGH
ÆMILIUS, *a noble Roman* ... GEOFFREY BAYLDON

A MESSENGER ... ... RON HADDRICK
YOUNG LUCIUS, *son to Lucius* PHILIP THOMAS
A NURSE ... ... ROSALIND ATKINSON
A CLOWN ... ... EDWARD ATIENZA
FIRST GOTH ... ... MERVYN BLAKE
SECOND GOTH ... ... DAVID KING
THIRD GOTH ... ... TRADER FAULKNER
PUBLIUS, *son to Marcus Andronicus* GABRIEL WOOLF
A ROMAN ... ... HUGH CROSS

Kinsmen of Titus, Priests, Judges, Soldiers, Huntsmen, Citizens and Goths:
JILL DIXON, ANN FIRBANK, DILYS HAMLETT, MARY LAW, NANCYE STEWART, RICHARD COE, PETER VAN GREENAWAY, ALAN HAYWOOD, ROBERT HUNTER, EMRYS JAMES, GEORGE LITTLE, REX ROBINSON, GEOFFREY SASSÉ, JOHN SOUTHWORTH, JOHN SPRINGETT, PAUL VIEYRA.

The play directed by PETER BROOK
Designs and Music by PETER BROOK
with
MICHAEL NORTHEN, DESMOND HEELEY, WILLIAM BLEZARD

BASSIANUS (*Act I Scene 1*)
Lord Titus, by your leave, this maid is mine

TITUS (*Act III Scene 1*) *Opposite*
When will this fearful slumber have an end?

DEMETRIUS (*Act II Scene 4*) *Above*
She hath no tongue to call, nor hands to wash

TITUS (*Act V Scene 3*) *Below*
For worse than Philomel you us'd my daughter,
And worse than Progne I will be reveng'd

Opposite
Anthony Quayle as Aaron, the Moor

Laurence Olivier as Titus Andronicus

Vivien Leigh as Lavinia

TITUS (*Act III Scene 1*) *Opposite*
. . . with our sighs we'll breathe the welkin dim,
And stain the sun with fog, as sometime clouds
When they do hug him in their melting bosoms

Alan Webb as Marcus Andronicus

Maxine Audley as Tamora

Peggy Ashcroft as Beatrice

Much Ado About Nothing

THE CONTINENT, LONDON AND THE PROVINCES 1955

The Play directed by JOHN GIELGUD
Scenery and Costumes designed by MARIANO ANDREU
Music composed by LESLIE BRIDGEWATER
Dances arranged by PAULINE GRANT

John Gielgud as Benedick

LEONATO, *Governor of Messina*	ANTHONY NICHOLLS
MESSENGER	JEREMY BURNHAM
BEATRICE, *niece to Leonato* ...	PEGGY ASHCROFT
HERO, *daughter to Leonato* ...	JUDITH STOTT
DON PEDRO, *Prince of Arragon*...	ANTHONY IRELAND
BENEDICK, *a young Lord of Padua*	JOHN GIELGUD
DON JOHN... ... ... *bastard brother to Don Pedro*	RAYMOND WESTWELL
CLAUDIO, *a young Lord of Florence*	RICHARD EASTON
CONRADE } *Followers of Don John* ...	MICHAEL MALNICK
BORACHIO } *Followers of Don John* ...	HAROLD LANG
ANTONIO, *brother to Leonato* ...	POWYS THOMAS
MARGARET } *Gentlewomen attending on Hero*	MOIRA LISTER
URSULA ... } *Gentlewomen attending on Hero*	HELEN CHERRY
PAGE TO BENEDICK ...	TIMOTHY HARLEY
BALTHAZAR, *Attendant to Don Pedro*	BEVERLEY CROSS
DOGBERRY, *a Constable* ...	GEORGE DEVINE
VERGES, *a Headborough*	DAVID O'BRIEN
WATCHMEN	JOHN GARLEY
WATCHMEN	DAVID MARLOWE
WATCHMEN	... PETER RETEY
WATCHMEN	NICHOLAS BRADY
FRIAR FRANCIS	PAUL HARDWICK
A SEXTON	... KEN WYNNE

Dancers, Servants, Wedding Guests:

JUNE BROWN, MARY WATSON, DAVID CONVILLE, BRIAN HANKINS, GARY RAYMOND, MICHAEL SPICE.

Left
Raymond Westwell as Don John and Anthony Ireland as Don Pedro

Below
Judith Stott as Hero, Helen Cherry as Ursula, Moira Lister as Margaret, Peggy Ashcroft as Beatrice

Right
Anthony Nicholls as Leonato
and Judith Stott as Hero

Below
George Devine as Dogberry
and David O'Brien as Verges

King Lear

THE CONTINENT, LONDON AND THE PROVINCES 1955

THE EARL OF KENT ...	ANTHONY NICHOLLS
THE EARL OF GLOUCESTER...	GEORGE DEVINE
EDMUND, *his bastard son* ...	HAROLD LANG
LEAR, *king of Britain*	JOHN GIELGUD
GONERIL, *eldest daughter to Lear*	HELEN CHERRY
THE DUKE OF ALBANY *her husband*	RAYMOND WESTWELL
REGAN, *second daughter to Lear*	MOIRA LISTER
THE DUKE OF CORNWALL ... *her husband*	ANTHONY IRELAND
CORDELIA, *youngest daughter to Lear*	PEGGY ASHCROFT *
THE DUKE OF BURGUNDY *Suitors to Cordelia*	PAUL HARDWICK
THE KING OF FRANCE *Suitors to Cordelia*	JEREMY BURNHAM
EDGAR, *elder son to Gloucester*	RICHARD EASTON
OSWALD, *steward to Goneril* ...	JOHN GARLEY
KNIGHT, *attending on Lear* ...	POWYS THOMAS
FOOL	DAVID O'BRIEN
CURAN, *a courtier*...	DAVID MARLOWE
SERVANTS TO CORNWALL	KEN WYNNE
	DAVID CONVILLE
	MICHAEL MALNICK
AN OLD MAN, *tenant to Gloucester*	PAUL HARDWICK
A DOCTOR...	PETER RETEY
A SOLDIER IN CORDELIA'S ARMY	MICHAEL SPICE
A CAPTAIN IN EDMUND'S ARMY	MICHAEL MALNICK
A HERALD...	BEVERLEY CROSS

Knights, Servants, Soldiers:
NICHOLAS BRADY, BRIAN HANKINS, TIMOTHY HARLEY, GARY RAYMOND.

* *The part of* CORDELIA *was played by* CLAIRE BLOOM *in London and by* MARY WATSON *in the Provinces*

The Play directed by GEORGE DEVINE
Scenery and Costumes designed by ISAMU NOGUCHI *Music and Sound-score composed by* ROBERTO GERHARD
Fights arranged by BERNARD HEPTON & JOHN GREENWOOD *Assistant to director on make-up* ALIX STONE
The photographs are by MARIA AUSTRIA *of Amsterdam*

Helen Cherry as Goneril and Raymond Westwell as Albany

Anthony Ireland as Cornwall and Moira Lister as Regan

GLOUCESTER (*Act IV Scene 6*) *Opposite*
The trick of that voice I do well remember

BURGUNDY (*Act I Scene I*) *Above*
I crave no more than what your highness offer'd

CORDELIA (*Act I Scene I*) *Below*
I know you what you are

LEAR (*Act II Scene 4*) *Opposite above*
Hysterica passio, down, thou climbing sorrow, Thy element's below!

LEAR (*Act I Scene 4*) *Opposite below*
Detested kite!
Thou liest

EDMUND (*Act V Scene 3*)
What you have charg'd me with,
that have I done

LEAR (*Act V Scene 3*)
Why should a dog, a horse, a rat, have life,
And thou no breath at all?

Hamlet

1956 SEASON

BARNARDO	PAUL VIEYRA
FRANCISCO	ROBERT ARNOLD
HORATIO	ANTHONY NICHOLLS
MARCELLUS	RON HADDRICK
THE GHOST *of Hamlet's father*	MARK DIGNAM
CLAUDIUS, *King of Denmark*	HARRY ANDREWS
GERTRUDE, *Queen of Denmark*	DIANA CHURCHILL
CORNELIUS } *Ambassadors*	PETER CELLIER
VOLTIMAND } *Ambassadors*	DAVID WILLIAM
LAERTES	ANDREW FAULDS
POLONIUS	GEORGE HOWE
HAMLET	ALAN BADEL
OPHELIA	DILYS HAMLETT
REYNALDO	PATRICK WYMARK
ROSENCRANTZ	JOHN GARLEY
GUILDENSTERN	EMRYS JAMES
THE FIRST PLAYER	CLIVE REVILL
PLAYER KING	JOHN MACGREGOR
PLAYER QUEEN	JUNE BROWN
DRUMMER	GILBERT COBBETT
FORTINBRAS	BASIL HOSKINS
A CAPTAIN	PETER CELLIER
LADIES *attending on the Queen*	VIRGINIA MASKELL, STEPHANIE BIDMEAD
ATTENDANTS	ALAN HAYWOOD, JOHN SOUTHWORTH
A SAILOR	PETER PALMER
A GRAVEDIGGER	PATRICK WYMARK
A CARPENTER	JOHN MACGREGOR
A PRIEST	GEORGE LITTLE
OSRIC	DAVID WILLIAM
A LORD	LEON EAGLES

Bishops, Lords, Attendants, Sailors, Players, Guards, Danes, Officers and Soldiers:
REX ROBINSON, ANTONY BROWN, THANE BETTANY, GORDON GARDNER, BRIAN MADISON, DEREK MAYHEW, JOHN SCOTT, MICHAEL TATE, RONALD WALLACE, BARRY WARREN.

The Play directed by MICHAEL LANGHAM
Scenery and lighting by MICHAEL NORTHEN *Costumes by* DESMOND HEELEY
Music by ALEXANDER GIBSON *Mime Play arranged by* LITZ PISK
Fight arranged by BERNARD HEPTON *and* JOHN GREENWOOD

Dilys Hamlett as Ophelia

George Howe as Polonius

Opposite
Alan Badel as Hamlet

CLAUDIUS (*Act I Scene 2*) *Above*
We have here writ to Norway, uncle of young Fortinbras . . .

HAMLET (*Act I Scene 5*) *Below*
Still am I call'd; unhand me gentlemen . . .

Opposite
Diana Churchill as Gertrude and Harry Andrews as Claudius

HAMLET (*Act III Scene 4*) *Opposite*
Confess yourself to heaven, Repent what's past, avoid what is to come . . . .

HAMLET (*Act III Scene 2*) *Above*
What, frighted with false fire?

OSRIC (*Act V Scene 2*) *Below*
A hit, a very palpable hit . . .

The Merchant of Venice

1956 SEASON

ANTONIO	Anthony Nicholls
SALERIO	Emrys James
SOLANIO	Robert Arnold
BASSANIO	Basil Hoskins
LORENZO	David William
GRATIANO	Andrew Faulds
PORTIA	Margaret Johnston
NERISSA	Prunella Scales
PAGE *to Portia*	Christopher Warby
BALTHASAR	George Little
SHYLOCK	Emlyn Williams
THE PRINCE OF MOROCCO	Mark Dignam
LAUNCELOT GOBBO	John Garley
OLD GOBBO	George Howe
LEONARDO	John Southworth
JESSICA	Jeannette Sterke
THE PRINCE OF ARRAGON	Clive Revill
STEPHANO	Paul Vieyra
SERVANT *to Antonio*	Alan Haywood
TUBAL	Ron Haddrick
SINGER	Rex Robinson
THE DUKE OF VENICE	George Howe
CLERK *of the Court*	Leon Eagles

Magnificoes of Venice, Officers, Attendants on Portia, Morocco and Arragon, and Citizens of Venice:
Stephanie Bidmead, June Brown, Virginia Maskell, Greta Watson, Peter Cellier, John MacGregor, Antony Brown, Thane Bettany, Gordon Gardner, Brian Madison, Derek Mayhew, Peter Palmer, John Scott, Michael Tate, Ronald Wallace, Barry Warren.

The Play directed by MARGARET WEBSTER
Scenery and costumes by ALAN TAGG *Music by* LESLIE BRIDGEWATER
Carnival Dance arranged by NORMAN AYRTON
Lighting by PETER STREULI

George Howe as Old Gobbo and John Garley as his son, Launcelot Gobbo

ANTONIO (*Act I Scene 3*) *Opposite*
Yes Shylock, I will seal unto this bond ..

(Act IV Scene 1)
Margaret Johnston as Portia
and Emlyn Williams as Shylock

PORTIA (*Act III Scene 2*) *Above*
Is it your dear friend that is thus in trouble?

Below *Anthony Nicholls as Antonio, with Jeannette Sterke and David William as Jessica and Lorenzo, Basil Hoskins and Margaret Johnston as Bassanio and Portia, Prunella Scales and Andrew Faulds as Nerissa and Gratiano*

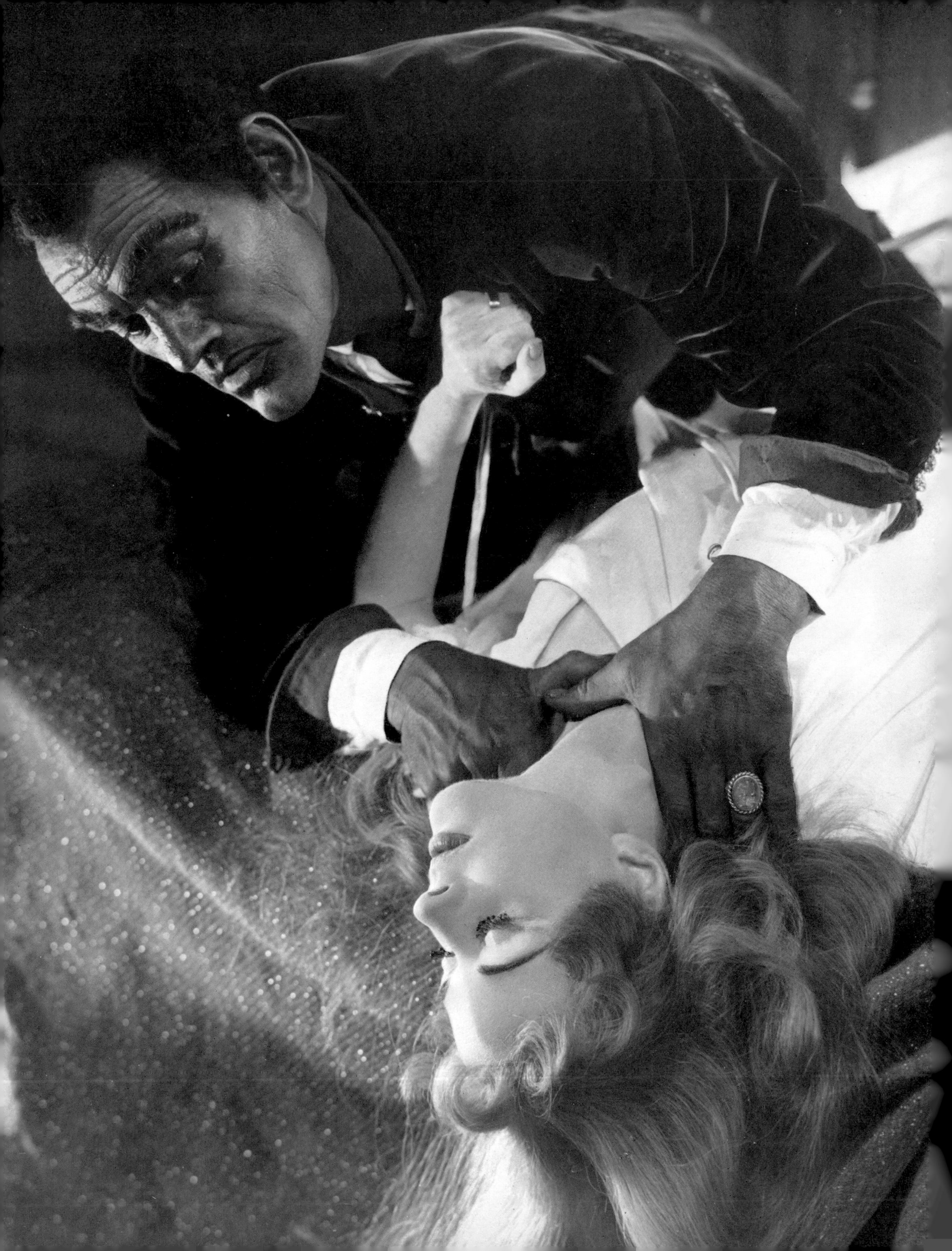

Othello

1956 SEASON

RODERIGO	JOHN GARLEY
IAGO	EMLYN WILLIAMS
BRABANTIO	ANTHONY NICHOLLS
OTHELLO	HARRY ANDREWS
CASSIO	BASIL HOSKINS
THE DUKE OF VENICE	MARK DIGNAM
LODOVICO	ANDREW FAULDS
SENATORS	DAVID WILLIAM, GEORGE LITTLE
DUKE'S OFFICERS	JOHN MACGREGOR, RONALD WALLACE
FIRST MESSENGER	LEON EAGLES
SECOND MESSENGER	MICHAEL TATE
DESDEMONA	MARGARET JOHNSTON
GRATIANO	TOBY ROBERTSON
MONTANO	RON HADDRICK
OFFICERS AT CYPRUS	PETER CELLIER, REX ROBINSON, ROBERT ARNOLD
EMILIA	DIANA CHURCHILL
HERALD	PETER PALMER
TRUMPETER	STANLEY WHEELER
CLOWN	PATRICK WYMARK
FIRST MUSICIAN	JOHN SOUTHWORTH
BIANCA	JEANNETTE STERKE

Senators, Officers, Soldiers, Servants, Musicians, Citizens of Cyprus:

STEPHANIE BIDMEAD, JUNE BROWN, DILYS HAMLETT, VIRGINIA MASKELL, PRUNELLA SCALES, GRETA WATSON, THANE BETTANY, ANTONY BROWN, GORDON GARDNER, ALAN HAYWOOD, EMRYS JAMES, BRIAN MADISON, DEREK MAYHEW, JOHN SCOTT, PAUL VIEYRA, BARRY WARREN, CHRISTOPHER WARBY

The Play directed by GLEN BYAM SHAW

Scenery and costumes by MOTLEY *Music by* ANTONY HOPKINS *Dance arranged by* PAULINE GRANT

Fight arranged by BERNARD HEPTON *and* JOHN GREENWOOD *Lighting by* PETER STREULI

EMILIA (*Act III Scene 3*)
Give me't again: poor lady,
she'll run mad When she shall lack it

(*Act V Scene 2*) *Opposite*
Harry Andrews as Othello
and Margaret Johnston as Desdemona

BRABANTIO (*Act I Scene 3*)
God bu'y, I ha' done. Please it your grace,
on to the state affairs

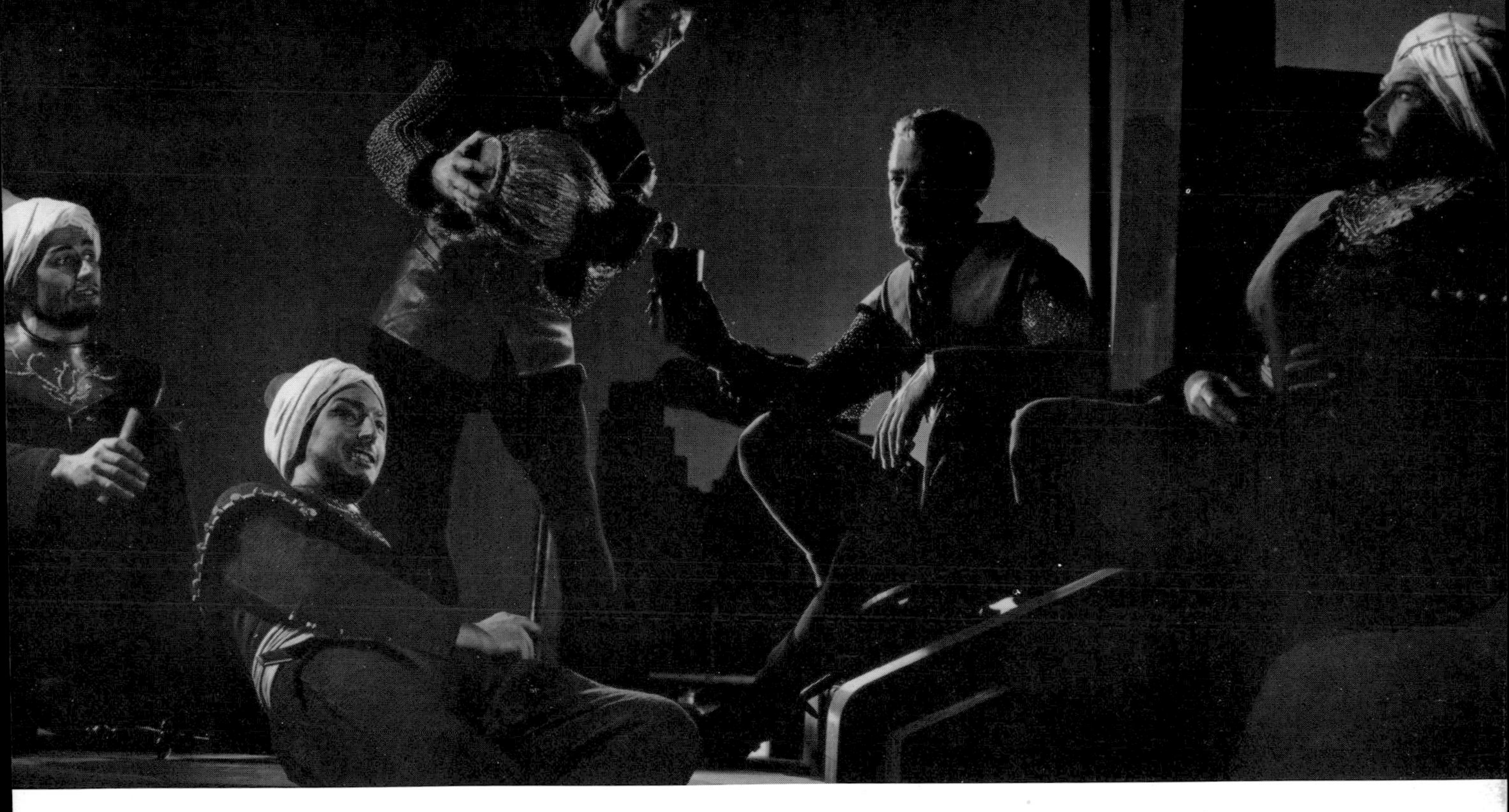

IAGO (*Act II Scene 3*) *Above*
A life's but a span; Why then let a soldier drink

OTHELLO (*Act IV Scene 1*) *Below*
I am glad to see you mad

IAGO (*Act III Scene 3*)
O, beware, my lord, of jealously;
It is the green-eyed monster . . .

BIANCA (*Act V Scene 1*) *Opposite*
O my dear Cassio! O my sweet Cassio!

Love's Labour's Lost

1956 SEASON

FERDINAND, *King of Navarre*		BASIL HOSKINS
LONGAVILLE	*Lords attending on the king*	ANDREW FAULDS
DUMAINE		DAVID WILLIAM
BEROWNE		ALAN BADEL
DULL, *a constable*		PATRICK WYMARK
COSTARD, *a rustic*		CLIVE REVILL
DON ADRIANO DE ARMADO, *a fantastical Spaniard*		HARRY ANDREWS
MOTH, *page to Armado* . .		RICHARD O'SULLIVAN
JAQUENETTA, *a country wench*		PRUNELLA SCALES
BOYET, *the Princess's chamberlain*		GEORGE HOWE
THE PRINCESS *of France* . .		GERALDINE McEWAN
A LORD		REX ROBINSON
MARIA . .	*Ladies attending on the Princess*	DILYS HAMLETT
KATHERINE		GRETA WATSON
ROSALINE		JEANNETTE STERKE
A FORESTER		PETER PALMER
HOLOFERNES, *a pedant* . .		MARK DIGNAM
SIR NATHANIEL, *a curate* . .		TOBY ROBERTSON
MERCADE, *a royal messenger* . .		PETER CELLIER

Scholars, Attendants, Countrymen and Countrywomen:
STEPHANIE BIDMEAD, VIRGINIA MASKELL, THANE BETTANY, ANTONY BROWN, GORDON GARDNER, RICHARD GREEN, ALAN HAYWOOD, BRIAN MADISON, DEREK MAYHEW, JOHN SCOTT, MICHAEL TATE, PAUL VIEYRA, RONALD WALLACE, BARRY WARREN.

The Play directed by PETER HALL
Scenery and costumes by JAMES BAILEY *Music by* RAYMOND LEPPARD
Dance arranged by PAULINE GRANT
Lighting by PETER STREULI

BEROWNE (*Act IV Scene 3*)
Guilty, my lord, guilty! I confess, I confess

PRINCESS (*Act V Scene 2*) *Opposite*
Sweet hearts, we shall be rich ere we depart

BEROWNE (*Act V Scene 2*) *Above*
Our states are forfeit, seek not to undo us

DULL (*Act IV Scene 2*) *Below*
I said the deer was not *a haud credo*, 'twas a pricket

DON ARMADO (*Act III Scene 1*) *Opposite*
Some enigma, some riddle: come, thy l'envoy begin

Measure for Measure

1956 SEASON

VINCENTIO, *the Duke*	Anthony Nicholls
ESCALUS	George Howe
ANGELO	Emlyn Williams
LUCIO	Alan Badel
TWO GENTLEMEN	Robert Arnold Leon Eagles
MISTRESS OVERDONE	Diana Churchill
POMPEY	Patrick Wymark
CLAUDIO	Emrys James
PROVOST	Mark Dignam
JULIET	Prunella Scales
FRIAR PETER	Toby Robertson
ISABELLA	Margaret Johnston
FRANCISCA	Stephanie Bidmead
ELBOW	John Garley
FROTH	John Southworth
A JUSTICE	George Little
TWO SOLDIERS	Alan Haywood Peter Cellier
A TROUBADOUR	Rex Robinson
MARIANA	Dilys Hamlett
ABHORSON	Ron Haddrick
A MESSENGER	Peter Palmer
BARNARDINE	Clive Revill

Officers, Soldiers, Nuns, Citizens and Prisoners:
June Brown, Virginia Maskell, Greta Watson, Thane Bettany, Antony Brown, Gordon Gardner, Richard Green, John MacGregor, Brian Madison, Derek Mayhew, Richard O'Sullivan, John Scott, Michael Tate, Paul Vieyra, Ronald Wallace, Barry Warren.

The Play directed by ANTHONY QUAYLE
Scenery and costumes by TANYA MOISEIWITSCH *Music by* LESLIE BRIDGEWATER
Lighting by MICHAEL NORTHEN

THE DUKE (*Act III Scene 1*)
Be absolute for death

ESCALUS (*Act III Scene 2*)
Go, away with her to prison!

(Act V Scene 1) Opposite
Anthony Nicholls as the Duke
Margaret Johnston as Isabella
Emlyn Williams as Angelo

ANGELO (*Act II Scene 4*)
. . . now I give my sensual race the rein

Opposite Above
POMPEY (*Act III Scene 2*)
You will not bail me then, sir?

Opposite Below
THE DUKE (*Act V Scene 1*)
Joy to you, Mariana! Love her, Angelo

Shakespeare Memorial Theatre

1953-4
LONDON AND THE CONTINENT
('Antony and Cleopatra')

Production Manager ..	..DESMOND HALL
Stage Director	.. PETER STREULI
Press and Public Relations	..JOHN GOODWIN
Costume Supervisor ..	.. KEGAN SMITH
Chief Construction Carpenter	FRED JENKINS
Property Master ..	.. GERRY WATTS
Scenic Artist	.. REG SAYLE
Stage Managers ..	BETTY CROWE JEAN ROBERTS
Assistant Stage Managers	KEITH GREENE MARK GOULLET
Stage Carpenter ..	EDDIE GOLDING
Chief Electrician ..	.. JOHN BRUCE
Wardrobe Master ..	.. JOE CLARK

1954
STRATFORD

Production Manager ..	..DESMOND HALL
Stage Director	.. PETER STREULI
House Manager ..	VAUGHAN KIMBER
Press and Public Relations	..JOHN GOODWIN
Catering Manageress ..	MRS. M. AVENELL
Box Office Manager ..	.. DAVID LYTTON
Costume Supervisor ..	.. KEGAN SMITH
Chief Construction Carpenter ..	FRED JENKINS
Property Master ..	.. GERRY WATTS
Scenic Artist	.. REG SAYLE
Stage Manager	.. ROY PARKER
Assistant Stage Managers	KEITH GREENE DAVID HARRIS HAL ROGERS JEAN WILKINSON
Stage Carpenter ..	EDDIE GOLDING
Chief Electrician ..	.. JOHN BRUCE
Wardrobe Mistress ..	MRS. A. SELLMAN

1955
STRATFORD

Production Manager ..	..DESMOND HALL
Stage Director	.. PETER STREULI
Assistant Stage Director	.. JEAN ROBERTS
House Manager ..	VAUGHAN KIMBER
Press and Public Relations	..JOHN GOODWIN
Assistant	VINCENT PEARMAIN
Catering Manageress ..	MRS M. AVENELL
Box Office Manager ..	.. DAVID LYTTON
Costume Supervisor ..	.. KEGAN SMITH
Chief Construction Carpenter ..	FRED JENKINS
Property Master ..	.. GERRY WATTS
Scenic Artist	.. REG SAYLE
Stage Managers ..	KEITH GREENE DAVID HARRIS
Assistant Stage Managers	HAL ROGERS MARGARET HILDER
Stage Carpenter ..	EDDIE GOLDING
Chief Electrician	.. JOHN BRUCE
Wardrobe Mistress ..	MRS A. SELLMAN

1955
THE CONTINENT, LONDON AND THE PROVINCES
('King Lear' and 'Much Ado about Nothing')

Manager and Stage Director	PATRICK DONNELL
Production Manager ..	..DESMOND HALL
Press and Public Relations	..JOHN GOODWIN
Assistant	VINCENT PEARMAIN
Costume Supervisor ..	.. KEGAN SMITH
Chief Construction Carpenter ..	FRED JENKINS
Property Master ..	.. GERRY WATTS
Scenic Artist	.. REG SAYLE
Stage Managers	MAURICE DANIELS MICHAEL HALLIFAX
Assistant Stage Managers	JANE SHIRLEY JEAN WILKINSON
Stage Carpenter ..	WILFRID HURWORTH
Wardrobe Mistress ..	.. LYNN HOPE

1956
STRATFORD

Assistant to the General Manager	PATRICK DONNELL
Production Manager ..	..DESMOND HALL
Stage Director	.. PETER STREULI
Assistant Stage Director	MAURICE DANIELS
House Manager ..	RICHARD TAYLOR
Press and Public Relations	..JOHN GOODWIN
Assistant	VINCENT PEARMAIN
Catering Manager ..	EDOARDO MILANO
Assistant Catering Manager ..	JEREMY GYE
Box Office Manager ..	.. JOHN JOLLEY
Costume Supervisor ..	.. KEGAN SMITH
Chief Construction Carpenter ..	FRED JENKINS
Property Master ..	.. GERRY WATTS
Scenic Artist	.. REG SAYLE
Stage Manager	.. JULIA SMITH
Assistant Stage Managers	HAL ROGERS ALISOUN BROWNE HOWARD BAKER
Stage Carpenter ..	EDDIE GOLDING
Chief Electrician ..	.. JOHN BRUCE
Wardrobe Mistress ..	MRS. A. SELLMAN

Music Adviser ..	..LESLIE BRIDGEWATER
Choreographer	.. PAULINE GRANT

THE THEATRE ORCHESTRA

Directed by	HAROLD INGRAM
Leader	.. CHARLES BYE